ILLUMINATIONS: A SERIES ON AMERICAN POETICS
Series Editor: Jon Thompson

ILLUMINATIONS: A SERIES ON AMERICAN POETICS
Series Editor: Jon Thompson

Illuminations focuses on the poetics and poetic practices of the contemporary moment in the USA. The series is particularly keen to promote a set of reflective works that include, but go beyond, traditional academic prose, so we take Walter Benjamin's rich, poetic essays published under the title of *Illuminations* as an example of the kind of approach we most value. Collectively, the titles published in this series aim to engage various audiences in a dialogue that will reimagine the field of contemporary American poetics. For more about the series, please visit its website at parlorpress.com/illuminations.

BOOKS IN THE SERIES

Xeno » Glossia: An Illuminated Study of Christine de Pizan by Marci Vogel
Countée Cullen's Harlem Renaissance: A Personal History by Kevin Brown
Things Are Completely Simple: Poetry and Translation by Brian Henry
The Poet's Tomb: The Material Soul of Poetry by Martin Corless-Smith
Vestiges: Notes, Responses, and Essays 1988–2018 by Eric Pankey
Sudden Eden by Donald Revell
Prose Poetry and the City by Donna Stonecipher

ALSO BY MARCI VOGEL

At the Border of Wilshire & Nobody
Death and Other Holidays

XENO » GLOSSIA

An Illuminated Study of Christine de Pizan

translations • inventions • interscriptions

Marci Vogel

Parlor Press
Anderson, South Carolina
www.parlorpress.com

Parlor Press LLC, Anderson, South Carolina, 29621

© 2025 by Marci Vogel
All rights reserved.
Printed in the United States of America
S A N: 2 5 4 - 8 8 7 9

Library of Congress Cataloging-in-Publication Data

Names: Vogel, Marci author
Title: Xeno glossia : an illuminated study of Christine de Pizan : translations, inventions, interscriptions / Marci Vogel.
Description: Anderson, South Carolina : Parlor Press, 2026. | Series: Illuminations: a series in American poetics | Includes bibliographical references. | Summary: "Compelled by the historical milieu, intriguing life story, and multi-faceted work of Late Medieval francophone poet Christine de Pizan, XENO GLOSSIA blends critical autotheory, multimodal translation, and interventionist poetics to advocate liberatory practices for twenty-first-century readers, thinkers, and makers of   language-and beyond"-- Provided by publisher.
Identifiers: LCCN 2025044824 (print) | LCCN 2025044825 (ebook) | ISBN 9781643175461 paperback acid-free paper | ISBN 9781643175478 adobe pdf | ISBN 9781643175485 epub
Subjects: LCSH: Christine, de Pisan, approximately 1364-approximately 1431--Criticism and interpretation | LCGFT: Literary criticism
Classification: LCC PQ1575.Z5 V64 2026 (print) | LCC PQ1575.Z5 (ebook)
LC record available at https://lccn.loc.gov/2025044824
LC ebook record available at https://lccn.loc.gov/2025044825

2 3 4 5

Cover design by Peter Figen.
Illustration of the author by Jaroslav Grodl.
Printed on acid-free paper.

Parlor Press, LLC is an independent publisher of scholarly and trade titles in print and multimedia formats. This book is available in paperback and ebook formats from Parlor Press on the World Wide Web at https://www.parlorpress.com or through online and brick-and-mortar bookstores. For submission information or to find out about Parlor Press publications, write to Parlor Press, 3015 Brackenberry Drive, Anderson, South Carolina, 29621, or email editor@parlorpress.com.

CONTENTS

Frontispiece [Here commences]   2
Invocation [A knock on the door . . .]   3
Incipit [The spade of inquiry]   5
Prelude [Arrival of the Departure]   7

BOOK I: OF HISTORIES [EARTHLY & CELESTIAL]   15

    Christine's « Vision » & the Economy of Writing as a Woman   17
    « venditions »   47
    Illuminated Histories   57
    « étoiles »   61

BOOK II: OF COUNTRIES [FAMILIAR & STRANGE]   81

    To Dream the Impossible Real: Christine's « Path » as
        Case Study in Medieval Dream Poetry   83
    « rêves »   105
    In the Country of Christine   117
    « tours »   123

BOOK III: OF KNOWINGS [GLOSSED & GLEANED]   143

    Inside the Tree of Battles: A Dendrochronology of « Deeds, Arms & Chivalry »   145
    « leavings »   165

BOOK IV: OF LANGUAGES [SILENT & VOICED]   191

    Translating Light   193
    « moëttes »   205
    « widow rounds »   209
    « interscriptions »   219
    « missives »   239

Envoi [My voice]   247
Explicit [A little song turned rhapsodic]   248
Colophon [Presence]   251

Dedication   252
Acknowledgements   253
Bibliography   257
About the Author   273

XENO » GLOSSIA

[*Here commences* . . . British Library MS Harley 4431, fol. 4r.]

A knock on the door by one whose hand glosses the pages

by turns stranger and familiar, the not from here and keeper of the hearth, *xenos* arrives as age-old friend or fearsome rival, blurred through a rain-soaked portal. Once named host, another guest, *xenos* summons shelter, sustenance, music of distant song. Whether guised as rough warrior or rouged face in the mirror, when *xenos* passes, you might yet glimpse immortal splendor. You might well recognize a more human, cautionary tale. The grizzled mariner's translation still inscribes the seawall: « To refuse mythic welcome harbors earthly wreckage. » When *xenos* opens her mouth to speak, light tumbles out. Only here, at the glimmering table of visitation, every tongue-bound marvel is spirited across—

Pinules: f. *Two small tablets in th' Albidada of an Astrolabe, hauing in them two little holes, through which the height of the Sunne, &c, is taken; some call them, the sights of th' Albidada.*

Pioche: f. *A little Pickax, or French Instrument of husbandrie, not much vnlike a Pickax; (and sometimes) also, as* Piot.

Piocher. *To dig, or breake vp the earth with a* Pioche.

Piocheur: m. *A digger, or breaker vp of the earth with a* Pioche; *and (more generally) any such labouring man.*

Piochon: m. *A little* Pioche.

Piolé: m. ée: f. *Spotted, or speckled; whence;* Riolé piolé. *Gaudie, or pide; also, diuersified, or set out with sundrie colours.*

Piolement: m. *The puling, or cheeping of Sparrowes, or young birds.*

Pioler. *To pule, cheepe, or chirpe, like a Sparrow, or yong bird.*

« Two small tablets in the alidade of an Astrolabe, through which the height of the Sun &c. is taken; Piocher is to dig; Pioler is to cheep, or chirp, like a sparrow, or young bird. »

[Randle Cotgrave's *French-English Dictionary*, 1611.]

Pren la pioche de ton entendement et fouis fort et fay grant fosse tout par tout ou tu verras les traces de ma ligne, et je t'aideray a porter hors la terre a mes propres espaules.[1]

Take the spade of your understanding & delve deeply

& hollow a channel around where you see

the traces of my plumb line & I will aide you bear out the earth

upon my own shoulders.

                                        I build my language out of rocks, I write, indeed,

                                        with the feeling of some scribe . . .[2]

                                        To scribe to make hear the words, to make sound

                                        the words, the words, the words made flesh.[3]

She went ahead, and I followed behind, and after we had arrived at the Field of Letters I began to excavate and dig, following her marks with the spade of inquiry. And this was my first work:

---

[1] *City of Ladies*, 8.1, trans. Vogel, Richards.
[2] Glissant, 43.
[3] Cha, 18.

[Lady in a Litter, *The Book of the Duke of True Lovers*, BnF, fr. 836, fol. 74v.]

ARRIVAL OF THE DEPARTURE: A PRELUDE

> *As I met her along the way with a very noble retinue, I approached her litter and greeted her, and she me.*[4]

Midway through the journey, I was on the train, tangled inside the pages of a book.[5] In translation: *To find in myself the possibility of the unexpected. To fall asleep a mouse and wake up an eagle! What delight! What terror.*[6] I was entering a new life, and the sentences flew across history, country, and language to convey the strangeness of leaving behind a state one knows well for the promise (only a promise!) of the possible. *What delight! What terror.* Transformation from one creature to another may be rare, but exhilarated trepidation in the face of metamorphosis is commonly human. There was nothing for it but to ride the train to its terminus, which, in my city, is the exact point where the line begins—at the edge of the sea.

≈

---

[4] *The Duke of True Lovers* in Willard, *Writings of Christine de Pizan*, trans. Fenster, 72.
[5] Dante, *The Inferno*, Canto I ll.1–3, trans. Pinsky.
[6] Cixous, *Coming to Writing*, 11.

From a Los Angeles hilltop, the Pacific Ocean curves into mountains. In its wide expanse drifts a promise: from the Latin *pacificus*: to make peace; related to *pact, an accord, alliance, a covenant*. Clear days, you can see Catalina Island. Very clear, the notch where two harbors meet.

Largest of the Earth's oceans—larger than all the Earth's lands put together—the Pacific also holds the greatest depth, the Mariana Trench, at over 36,000 feet. If Mount Everest were plopped into the deepest point, its summit would remain submerged a mile under the surface of the sea.[7]

Named for the Austrian-born Spanish queen who funded a seventeenth-century missionary voyage to the New World, the Mariana Trench is home to one of the largest single-celled organisms on the planet. Neither animal, nor plant, nor fungus, these extraordinary creatures—called *Xenophyophora*—host a kaleidoscopic array of infinitesimal marine life.[8] In exchange, they extract various minerals and sediments from their abyssal surroundings to construct hard shells biologists call *tests*. The term—which derives from the Latin *testa*—refers not to examination, as in *testimony*, but to shape, as in a *rounded bowl, amphora*, or *bottle*.

---

[7] "Cameron's Long Way Down," National Geographic Society, 2012.
[8] "Researchers Identify Mysterious Life Forms in the Extreme Deep Sea," Scripps Institution of Oceanography, 2011.

Found in all the world's oceans—and in the watery depths of the Mariana Trench at six and a half miles underneath—xenophyophores are named after the diverse elements that comprise their exoskeleton tests, the vessels in which they live: *xenophyophora*, from the Greek, meaning *bearer of foreign bodies.*

≈

It's said Magellan christened the Earth's largest body of water *Mar Pacifico* upon encountering peaceful winds during his attempt to circumnavigate the world in 1521. For two centuries, the ocean was often called the *Sea of Magellan*. One country called it a *Mare clausum*—a sea closed to others. Forty-two sovereign nations are listed as bordering the Pacific's waters. When does an age of discovery become one of dominion? How does a pact become broken?

Which might also be to ask: How is an explorer different from a pilgrim?
A: *Pilgrims*, writes Anne Carson, *were people wondering, wondering. Whom shall I meet now?* [9]

---

[9] Carson, *Plainwater*, 133.

In a deep-sea ecosystem of the Pacific, the meeting of disparate elements creates an abode to shelter the most remote, the most minute, of life forms. *Walking dancing, pleasure: these accompany the poetic act.*[10] Which might also be to say: Even when our companions are unseen, we're never alone in the presence of making.

≈

Virgil may be among the most ancient of companions, but it was the Cumaean Sibyl who led Virgil through the underworld. The sun god Phoebus Apollo is said to have consigned her to an eternal life of aging when she refused his advances.[11] An unwelcome alliance can raise a stormy sea.

It can also block safe passage. In Greek mythology, a winged monster with a woman's head, a lion's body, and a serpent's tail is said to have settled on a cliff just outside the walled city of Thebes. Known as the Sphinx, the treacherous sentinel posed the same lethal riddle to all who wanted to travel through the city gates: "What creature is it that walks on four feet in the morning, on two at noon, and on three in the evening?"[12] Nobody dared enter or leave for fear of being devoured.

---

[10] Cixous, "The School of Dreams" in *Three Steps on the Ladder of Writing*, trans. Sellars, 64.
[11] Ovid, *Metamorphosis*, XIV.151, trans. Martin.
[12] D'Aulaire's *Book of Greek Myths*, 158–60.

It was a stranger, finally, who freed the trapped populace when he guessed the correct answer: "It is man. As a child, he crawls on four. When grown, he walks upright on his two feet, and in old age he leans on a staff." The citizens were so grateful, they made the stranger king.

A. *Pilgrims were people who loved a good riddle.*[13]

≈

The companions who accompany me near the edge of the Pacific are neither divine nor immortal, monster or king, but historical and imagined—and all the more welcome for steadfast guidance, constant through centuries and all weathers, on land and at sea.

Among my provisions: Key, notebook, pen. *Pilgrims were people who carried little. They carried it balanced on their heart.*[14]

Pilgrim: Old French for *crusader, foreigner, stranger*; by way of Latin, *from abroad, the acre beyond.* To translate is *to carry across*, as a pilgrim might.

---

[13] Carson, *Plainwater*, 125.
[14] Carson, *Plainwater*, 187.

Or a guide, pointing to possible directions.

A: *. . . the only rule of travel is, Don't come back the way you went. Come a new way.*[15]

≈

To walk is a miracle of ambulation. It requires a mobility often taken for granted. Even for those accustomed to transport by foot, physicality is a temporary condition—feet will blister, knees won't hold out forever. Arthritis, accident, age. Recall the Sphinx's riddle, the Sibyl's withering body in her ampulla shelter.

Injury or dislocation take us out of our customary mode—as do unknown sentences finding us on a train. Or language newly made, *bearer of foreign bodies.*

In order to write at all, counsels Hélène Cixous in "The School of Dreams," *something must be displaced, starting with the bed. One has to get going.*[16] Sometimes one gets going by way of stopping; of not continuing as usual, but as strange.

Maybe to uphold the pact is not to keep the peace, but to upend the ship on which it sails. Which might also be to wander off a long-mapped course, *wondering, wondering whom shall I meet now?*

---

[15] Carson, *Plainwater*, 123.
[16] Cixous, *Three Steps on the Ladder of Writing*, trans. Sellars, 65.

The language of poetry, writes Lyn Hejinian, *is a language of inquiry, not the language of genre.*[17]

Q. How does an inquiry differ from an inquisition?
A. *We walk, side by side, in different countries.*[18]

We depart as pilgrims, companions, wanderers, carrying little. On our breaking hearts, endless arrivals.

In the deepest of waters, we make a new home.

≈

---

[17] Hejinian, *The Language of Inquiry*, 2.
[18] Carson, *Plainwater*, 131.

BOOK I
OF HISTORIES [EARTHLY & CELESTIAL]

[« First, Christine tells how her spirit was transported. » *Le Livre de la vision de Christine*. BnF, fr. 1176, fol. 1r.]

CHRISTINE'S « VISION » & THE ECONOMY OF WRITING AS A WOMAN

> *... language may be one of the many elements that allow us to make sense of things, of ourselves*[19]

> *The segments of untranslatability are scattered through the text, making the translation a drama, and the wish for a good translation a wager.*[20]

This is a story about trading in language, a story of sale and purchase, acquisition and acquiescence. It's a story knit of female voices, past and present, each creating (and recreating) the other in turn. It begins with words found in history, and continues in a telling that plays for keeps. This is a story earned from wanting. Translation is its purveyor; invention, its currency.

◊

---

[19] Spivak, "The Politics of Translation" in *Outside in the Teaching Machine*, 179.
[20] Ricoeur, *On Translation*, trans. Brennan, 5.

To sell in French is *vendre*, and the *vendition* of the Middle Ages was a lyrical form in dialogue, in which the first line begins with the speaker offering something for sale. The partner then improvised a versified answer, rhyming with the object sold.[21] The exchange was intended as an amusing game of clever flirtation.

Sometime around 1400, an Italian-born woman living in France composed a sequence of nearly seventy *venditions*, titled *Jeux à vendre* in the comprehensive 1886 volume of her works edited by Maurice Roy.[22] *Jeux à vendre* translates as "Games for Sale," but for Christine de Pizan, money was no game. Often credited as the first woman to earn a living through writing, Christine well understood the desperation of financial hardship.

The daughter of a court astrologer, Christine was of a noble class, but after the deaths of her father and husband, the 25-year-old widow undertook responsibility for supporting her mother and three young children. A niece was also left in her care. Christine might have married again, but she chose not to. As was the case with most unattached women of her historical time and place, Christine's security—both financial and sexual—was precarious.

---

[21] *The Distaff Gospels*, 24-25, n.3.
[22] *Œuvres Poétiques*, vol. 1, 187–205.

She was left with a wealth of unscrupulous creditors and scant protection against reputation-blackening rumor.

Completed in 1405, *Christine's Vision* provides an astonishingly candid first-person account of Christine's dire straits following the untimely death of her husband, who had earned a steady income as a notary for the king: "Then troubles arose from all sides, and as is the common fare of widows, lawsuits and legal disputes came to me from everywhere. . . ."[23]

Likening herself to a "captain of a ship lost in the storm," Christine writes of the lengths required to keep her fledgling family afloat. She writes of betrayed trust. Of the shame of being found in want. Of the humiliation of asking for help.

Christine writes with surprising modernity about the bitterness of marital and material loss, but perhaps most remarkably, she openly confides the high cost required of widowed discretion:

> Oh God, how many annoying remarks, I had to listen to; how many stupid looks, how many jokes from some fat drunkard did I suffer; and because I was afraid of putting my case at risk and was so dependent on its

---

[23]*Christine's Vision* in *Selected Writings of Christine de Pizan*, trans. Blumenfeld-Kosinski, 173–201.

outcome, I hid my thoughts and turned away without answering, or else I pretended that I did not understand, and that I took it all as a light joke.[24]

Whatever bargain she struck with politic silence to avoid personal bankruptcy, Christine publicly expresses her outrage in *Vision*. She censures the routine misogyny running roughshod through sovereign domain and holds to account an entire kingdom of "worthy and valiant men" who do nothing to intervene with unjust laws and harassment "by the powerful." Drawing on her own early poetry, Christine summarily faults nobles, clerks, princes, knights, prelates, judges, and officials as she exercises sole proprietorship over the single asset she owns free and clear: her voice.

◊

Yet language is not everything. It is only a vital clue to where the self loses its boundaries.[25]

◊

---

[24] *Vision*, trans. Blumenfeld-Kosinski, 190.
[25] Spivak, 180.

In her 1993 groundbreaking essay, "The Politics of Translation," Gayatri Chakravorty Spivak reworks Walter Benjamin's 1923 terminology to propose that "[t]he task of the feminist translator is to consider language as a clue to the workings of gendered agency."[26]

For Spivak, this task includes facilitating a "love between the original and its shadow, a love that permits fraying," whereby "the translator earns permission to transgress from the trace of the other—before memory—in the closest places of the self."[27]

It's not linguistic prowess that's solicited in translation then, but the warp and woof of the text—its language and the limits of that language, which "point at the silence . . . the absolute fraying. . . ."[28] In translating the Middle French of Christine's *venditions*, these silences and frayings unfolded glimmerings of another's voice.[29] I called her Sylvie at first—bits of shine blazing a dark-wood path—but knew I hadn't yet earned license to name.

In the legacy of Christine, a wholesale investment would need to be made.

---

[26] Spivak, 179.
[27] Spivak, 180–81.
[28] Spivak, 183.
[29] Ricoeur refers to "opening out the folds" in *On Translation*, trans. Brennan, 5.

In the language of Spivak, "surrender to the text" is the suitable remittance for such a claim: "If you want to make the translated text accessible," she advises, "try doing it for the person who wrote it."[30]

Across history, country, and economies, Christine and I shared an ardent desire for language we did not yet possess. If we were dealing in love, surrender seemed a bargain.

◊

As did Christine, I gave myself over to a vast library, not of a king, but of the university funding my apprenticeship. As collateral, I offered good-faith effort, resolute perseverance, and countless hours, all very un-billable. I scoured borrowed tomes of war, schism, upheaval; ran my fingers along gilded branches of royal family trees, pricked my thumb on a porcupine needle, symbol of Louis d'Orléans, murdered by order of his cousin, Jean the Fearless, tipping a fraught kingdom into civil war. Arch political rivals, both dukes were nephews to a man whose enormous wealth financed many of the most resplendent manuscripts of the fifteenth century:

---

[30] Spivak, 190–91.

[January. *Très Riches Heures du duc de Berry*, illuminated by the Limbourg Brothers, 1412-1416. « The Duke, in blue, is seated to the right of the feast table laden with the New Year delicacies and gifts traditionally exchanged by men at court. » Bibliothèque du château de CHANTILLY, 0065 (1284) 1v.]

I abandoned myself not only to texts paper, vellum, and digital, but to the three-dimensional fabric of Christine's time, place, and culture. I scrolled away hours over facsimile chronicles of a chivalric historian, wrecked my eyes on the small-type observations of an anonymous citizen.[31]

---

[31] Jean Froissart's detailed prose account of the Hundred Years' War is preserved in more than 150 manuscripts, many illuminated. Composed by an unidentified author, *Le Journal d'un bourgeois de Paris* chronicles politics, war, and life in Paris between 1405 and 1450.

Every afternoon of a leaf-fall season, I walked along the Seine's edge in a distant village little changed by the passage of centuries. Transported, I stood on the cathedral floor where Christine once attended midnight mass. Inside a castle now a museum, my twenty-first century device photographed (without flash) the bejeweled scepter of the wealthy king who had brought Christine's family from Bologna to Paris sometime around 1368. Hundreds of years into the future, I took a turn in the City of Lights where Christine first illuminated her manuscripts into history; stood in a rainy queue to purchase a ticket to the Saint Chapelle pictured in the Duke's *Très Riches Heures*; was put on a plane back to LAX when my passport went missing.

And yet none of this, not even the loss of bureaucratic identity, involved surrender of any genuine value. Linguistically speaking, such actions were more akin **to taking**—*prendre*—rather than, as the Old French root *rendre* denotes, **to give back, present, yield; give in, exchange, restore, repair; keep, fulfill (as with a promise)**. Indeed, during the late fourteenth century in which Christine traded one language for another, the etymon might have been used to mean **repeat, say again, recite; translate**.

In other words," writes Spivak, *"if you are interested in talking about the other, and/or in making a claim to be the other, it is crucial to learn other languages."*[32]

I'd entered the university as a first-generation undergraduate, returning to study poetry after many years as a teacher in the language of children. It had been decades since high school French with the elegant Mme. Williamson, who swapped dogeared textbooks for *Paris Match* and never spoke in English. A good bit of freshman year ticked past before I could decipher much more than photographs in those glossy magazines, and yet they remained more palpable in memory than the language of academe in which I now found myself as a poet. Keenly aware of this intrinsic estrangement—and the university's considerable investment in the education of a later-in-life student—I worked hard to make up gaps, to prove worthy of endowed tuition.

And yet, parsing Spivak's text from a library-provided PDF, it became clear that what most needed surrender was the exact holding I'd worked hardest to gain—currency in the language of scholarship—for intimacy with Christine's. Only in exchanging rhetorical fluency for tender skin in the game might I earn the "right

---

[32] Spivak, 192.

to become [an] intimate reader."[33] Only by rending my own silvered tongue, might Christine's pages yield to love's fraying. Only then might the glimmering voice speak her true name.

◊

Christine earned her living, finally—and the legacy by which we still know her—by setting upon an intensive course of study and producing her own illuminated manuscripts, which in the manner of medieval economy, she offered as gifts to those wealthy enough to reward her with monetary compensation. By her own reckoning, Christine "compiled fifteen major works . . . contained in seventy large-size quires" between 1399 and 1405, when she records the account in her *Vision*.[34] Several of these came to rest among the duke of Berry's library treasures.

One of those works, *The Book of the City of Ladies*, remains among her most famous. In it, Christine catalogues estimable women through the ages, telling their stories "to confront head-on the tradition of literary misogyny . . . that pervaded her

---

[33] Spivak, 183.

[34] *Vision*, 194. Contemporary biographer Charlotte Cooper-Davis notes that "over a career of almost four decades," Christine composed "around thirty major works . . . that survive in over two hundred manuscripts. . . .[E]ven more remarkable, is that [Christine] oversaw the production of fifty-four of her manuscripts herself and several of them are written in her own hand."

culture."[35] Brick by brick, she constructs an unshakable foundation of valor and resistance, recasting archaic narratives so that formerly discredited female figures might receive their long-due merit. Even the cost of the original trespass—eternal banishment for earthly knowledge—gains added value under Christine's balance sheet: "Humankind has now become one with God which never would have happened if Eve hadn't sinned."[36]

Another woman refunded the full measure of her standing in Christine's *City of Ladies* is the Cumaean sibyl, Almethea. Ovid's version, with which Christine was familiar, reduces the sibyl to perpetual deterioration in an ampulla prison after the prophetic virgin dares spurn the advances of a god. It's the same story I know from Charles Martin's 2004 prize-winning translation of the *Metamorphoses*. Without such translations, I might not know the story at all, but for all my schooling, Christine's telling is the first I ever read of an author who burns her own books after being denied fair payment for their worth.

Only when Almethea lays out her plan to torch the entire lot—three volumes each day of refusal—does the tyrannical king acquiesce to "the price which she had first demanded" for the remaining books. While the expenditure remains

---

[35] Brown-Grant, introduction to *The Book of the City of Ladies*, xvii.
[36] *City*, I.9. trans. Brown-Grant, 23.

unspecified, it proves a wise dealing as Christine details exactly how (with a holy guarantor no less) the Sybil's books will yield unforeseen dividends:

> Now, pay attention here, dear friend, and consider how God bestowed such great favor on a single woman who possessed the insight to counsel and advise not only one emperor during his lifetime but also, as it were, all those who were to come in Rome as long as the world lasts, as well as to comment upon all the affairs of the empire. Tell me then, please, where was there ever a man, who did this?[37]

Should any further question linger, Christine—well-versed in a long line of literary players—concludes her recounting so that readers understand fully their ongoing debt to a woman: "Virgil speaks in verse about this sibyl in his book. She ended her days in Sicily and for a long time afterward her tomb was shown to visitors." Such does a final sentence provide lasting redress against those whose greed left a writer like Christine in want.

---

[37] *City*, II.3. trans. Richards, 102–04.

◊

In translating Christine's *venditions*, I was greedy *with* want. I wanted words to yield riches, afford more than one meaning, revel in ambiguity. Linguistic proficiency was no longer enough. I wanted a poet's agility, an abundance of language born of surrender to reading. Christine's sibyl burns her books when a king does not pay her asking price. I almost stole a book to translate Christine's verses—a dictionary, a very expensive one, loaned from another university's library. The loan was up, and I still needed the book, and I thought I might say the book was lost, pay only the fine, which was less than the cost of the book, even with the breath of others marking the pages.

At first, the lie was in good faith—the book *was* lost; I'd left it in the backseat of my car for weeks—hours given over to paid employment, no time to dally with words, the usual supply-chain blockage, a skewed distribution of resources. Winter break, my mother visited from Arizona, as she does every year since she moved from California to live near her sisters in a state where retirement doesn't yet cost the remaining years of a life's savings. I emptied the car to make room, placed the book somewhere I no longer remembered.

The book came due, and I thought to pay the fine quickly, have done with the guilt. Then, as if by some magic trick, the book appeared, a shiny penny on the sidewalk others pass, but only you see. I thought to steal it newly recovered, but figured Christine would never condone such a theft. My own university's librarian, a woman born into a language other than English, ordered a copy for keeps. I may keep it forever. I have it still, prized spine at my desk.

◊

Regarding the discursive appearance of mothers, Christine makes recurring mention of hers, a "worthy" and "dignified" woman lauded in Christine's *Vision* as the first of Christine's greatest treasures: "[N]ever was she overcome by any tribulations, nor did impatience ever break her courageous heart. . . . Just think what a great favor God is doing you by letting such a noble woman, so filled with virtue, live to old age in your company." If Christine had been discontented at the start of her narrative because she could not "provide for her [mother] as is fitting," by its conclusion, she arrives at an understanding that "this desire when coupled with patience, is commendable for both [Christine and her mother]."[38]

---

[38] *Vision*, trans. Blumenfeld-Kosinski, 199.

It's not expedient fulfillment of material desire that holds value, Christine's Philosophy seems to counsel, but enduring commitment to values that hold true, no matter how poor the cards Lady Luck doles out. Recognizing the rare insight attained through trying circumstance, Christine crowns the labor of her *Vision* with three precious gemstones: a diamond, "its great virtue does not vanish"; a cameoed jewel; and a "ruby, clear and bright and without blemish, which has the property of becoming more and more pleasing the more one looks at it."[39] In Christine's *Vision*, sound discernment requires a finely attuned eye, and misguided buyers beware counterfeit aims.

Early in my study, my own highly worthy, much cherished (and ever-mindful of finances) mother had asked, *What did Christine do when someone who promised to pay for a manuscript didn't?* I hadn't yet read about the sibyl's incendiary act of rebellion, but I did learn this: One of Christine's most wealthy patrons, Jean the Fearless, was repeatedly late with payment, and when Christine needed to secure a placement for her son's future, Jean's equally well-heeled cousin, Louis of Orléans proved less than forthcoming with assistance.

---

[39] *Vision*, trans. Blumenfeld-Kosinski, 201.

In fact, both royals failed Christine in the safe return of her son, Jean de Castel, from England after she entrusted him to the care of the Earl of Salisbury. The Earl lost his head in a royal coup, and when the new king, Henry IV, not only insisted Jean remain at court but entreated Christine "with generous promises" to join them, she was left to deploy a mother's crafty bargaining acumen: "I dissembled and thanked the king, saying that I was at his command, all this in order to get my son back. . . . I went to great trouble and sent some of my books so that my son finally got leave to come and accompany me . . . a trip which I have not yet made."[40]

Christine never did leave her adopted home, even as its rulers abandoned their own lands to corruption, injustice, and the ravages of war. Instead, she embarked on a sweeping recalculation of what it meant to write as a woman. Along with the language of another country, Christine gained fluency with an immutably male chorus to emerge with an entirely new voice—one she wielded across stations, whether in appeal or resistance. "Once a man criticized my desire for knowledge by saying that it was not fitting for a woman to possess learning because there was so little of it," she writes in her *Vision*. "I replied that it was even less fitting for a man to possess ignorance because there was so much of it."[41] Christine may or

---

[40] *Vision*, trans. Blumenfeld-Kosinski, 195.
[41] *Vision*, trans. Blumenfeld-Kosinski, 193.

may not have possessed Ovid's Greek well enough to translate it into the French of her time, but she certainly altered the terms of the exchange.

The woman who risked all she had—and all she didn't—so that she might collect the rightful inheritance of her voice fulfilled the promise of desire with steadfast patience, tremendous effort, and savvy determination. She allied herself with wisdom, defied misogynistic tradition, and foraged a brilliant education out of "small coins and bits of change . . . fallen from the great wealth" of her father's extensive store of knowledge.[42] Book by book, she established her own authority, even as she strategically undercut it in service to far-sighted aims.

In her *Book of Fortune's Transformation* of 1403, Christine characterizes herself as "simple and of small intelligence," a vulnerable widow shipwrecked by grief. At the same time, she refuses to "be silent about the good or the bad things [she] has to say," and resolves to "tell all that there is to tell," including a vivid first-person account of "how from being a woman I became a man."[43] Modeling her extraordinary transformation after Ovid's gender-fluid tales of Tiresias and Iphis, Christine describes the process by which Fortune "my mistress . . . palpitated and

---

[42] *The Book of Fortune's Transformation*, trans. Blumenfeld-Kosinski, 95. Blumenfeld-Kosinski's essay "Christine de Pizan and the Misogynistic Tradition" appears on pages 297–311.
[43] *Fortune's Transformation*, trans. Blumenfeld-Kosinski, 89–91.

took in her hands each bodily part" until Christine "became a true man (this is no fable), capable of taking charge of the ship. Fortune taught me this trade and I set myself to work in this context."[44]

In every context, and in whatever guise she appeared (typically a blue gown and white headdress), Christine wrote to be read in a time, place, and culture where most women did not—could not. Christine could, and she did. Challenging Fortune at her own game, she wrote not only of her own life, but of others without the same chance. She wrote of maidens, wives, widows, princesses and prostitutes. She wrote of martyrs and saints, those who suffered grave mishandling, and those unafraid to strike a match.

More than that, Christine frayed the stories that had always been told, "graduated into speaking," as Spivak might say, "of intimate matters in the language of the original,"[45] thereby transforming the language she acquired as a young girl more profoundly than if she had translated it into her mother's Italian. She transformed, too, the physical manifestation of that language, producing her own manuscripts and employing at least one woman to illuminate them.[46] Rather than burning her

---

[44] *Fortune's Transformation*, trans. Blumenfeld-Kosinski, 106–07.
[45] Spivak, 187.
[46] Christine's illuminator, Anastasie, is identified in Margolis' *An Introduction to Christine de Pizan*, 74.

work, Christine took her "tools and hammer on the anvil . . . durable as iron . . . to forge [books that] will for all time to come keep [her] memory alive before the princes and the whole world. . . ."[47] We are still reading the gifts of that labor, those gambles in language.

◊

In modern French, the word *jeu* translates as **a game**, or, if we are speaking of the theater, **to act**, as in **play a part**. It can also refer to **gambling**. *Cacher son jeu* is **to keep one's cards hidden** or **conceal one's hand**. *En jeu* points to **what's at stake**.

For Spivak, what's at stake in "The Politics of Translation" is not a single equivalency of meaning, but agency, "the production of identity . . . as pluralized as a drop of water under a microscope."[48] My own desire had not been simply a poet's desire for words—for multiplicity—but a promissory note for the task ahead. As translators with a vested interest in restoring agency in and around language, "[w]e must attempt," as Spivak notes, "to enter . . . as one directs a play,

---

[47] *Vision*, trans. Blumenfeld-Kosinski, 193–94.
[48] Spivak, 179.

as an actor interprets a script. That takes a different kind of effort from taking translation to be a matter of synonym, syntax and local colour."[49]

In the dictionary I almost stole, the *jeu* of Old French also translates as **a game** or **sport**. If you follow the game all the way through, *jeu* leads to *jou*, which arrives, finally, at *je*, as in the singular pronoun **I**. **I'm for sale**, whispers Christine's title, not unlike Cole Porter's down-on-her-luck singer, advertising her wares.

In the dictionary I almost stole, *jeu* is defined as **a love poem in dialogue form**, but *jou* also renders the following: **yoke, bond, and join**. Exactly *who* is doing the joining remains in play. **Jousting** and **sex** are also in the entry's mix, as if in struggle with **jest**, as if to resist any notion that these verses are just a game.

In surrendering to the text, in reading as a translator, part of the task, as Spivak posits, is to uncover "a history of that refusal and resistance. . . . It is therefore only appropriate that its conclusion should gesture towards the limit, risk the re-inversion of the boundary by speaking from the other, refusing silence to what is unsaid."[50]

---

[49] Spivak, 181–82.
[50] Spivak quotes from Peter de Bolla's *The Discourse of the Sublime: Readings in History, Aesthetics, and the Subject*, 200.

In the dictionary I almost stole, *jeu* can also mean: **to propose an alternative**.

◊

Threatened by increasing violence unchecked by rulers with desires more unscrupulous than ardent, Christine fled Paris and her public writing life for the cloistered sanctuary where she remained in protective exile until her death. While sequestered, Christine wrote what is believed to be the first poem to narrate the triumph of a young Joan of Arc. With the exception of one other manuscript, no other writings from these final years of Christine's life are thought to exist.

The scholar part of my (pluralized) identity isn't particularly interested in disproving this claim. The poet part, however, aches when she imagines another who paid such a steep price for her voice remaining silent the last decade of her life. And the (not so) secret agent who acts as translator for a woman who inscribed loss with brilliance *refuses* to register an absence of words as forfeiture of speech.

No, the farther I surveilled over pixilated centuries, the closer I examined those digitized manuscripts, the more clearly I detected pages glossed with invisible ink.

In the task of Christine, maybe translation required a sibylline flame for the illuminated whole to take shape.

Spivak speaks to those gaps in translation "where meaning hops into spacy emptiness between two named historical languages," those breaks in the rhetorical surface where "we feel the selvedges of the language-textile give way, fray into *frayages* or facilitations." It's our habitual "stake in agency" that "keeps the fraying down to a minimum," Spivak observes, "except in the communication and reading of and in love."[51] Maybe those scholarly gaps I'd been trying to make up were not lack, but indicators of another knowledge—call it love, call it a glimmering, call it poetry.

As any English-language dictionary will relay, the word *poet* comes from a Greek root meaning *to make*. In any identity, I wanted "to make sense of things," as Spivak says—which is also to say that in surrendering to Christine's text, I wanted to make sense of myself and the increasingly precarious world I share with 8 billion fellow humans and exponentially more vulnerable beings.

---

[51] Spivak, 180. Ricoeur also discusses the *textures* and *weave* of sequences, 27.

I'm well past the age Christine was when she entered her long passage of unwritten folios. Fortune, fate, and government-subsidized health insurance has let my mother reach octogenarian wisdom, if not directly in my company, within a half-day's drive. In the long game of what we hold dear, *en jeu* skips over what's **at play** to what's **at stake**.

Six centuries after Christine's *Vision*, there remain deep inequities of education, opportunity, choices and freedoms—indelible gashes that cut across language, geography, and political bodies. Crushing poverty continues to be borne by labor robbed of justice, and corrosive powers continue to reign over economies that lay claim to wealth gained at irreconcilable expense. Even as I write, declarations against tyranny and oppression are trading in futures that would elect terms of transgression over the inalienable right to be an intimate reader.[52] *What's at stake?*

"There is no document of civilization which is not at the same time a document of barbarism," wrote Walter Benjamin not long before fleeing certain murder in

---

[52] See, for example: "Abraham Lincoln called [the Declaration of Independence] a rebuke to tyranny and oppression." https://www.archives.gov/founding-docs/declaration; "Public Libraries Saw 92 Percent Increase in Number of Titles Targeted for Censorship Over the Previous Year [2023 compared to 2022]." https://www.ala.org/news/2024/03/american-library-association-reports-record-number-unique-book-titles; "Grab 'em by the pussy. You can do anything." https://www.nytimes.com/2016/10/08/us/donald-trump-tape-transcript.html

a country that had once promised shelter.⁵³ Faced with the threat of return, Benjamin took his own life. *What's at stake?* It's a textbook question of rhetoric, but it's not a rhetorical question.

Well aware of my own muddied skirt in the marketplace of documents, I bid one response on behalf of a single microscopic pluralized self; a finite life on an ailing planet; a poet and translator; a mother's daughter who entered the university's library as a first-generation scholar and emerged with knowledge entrusted to the children of others. What's *en jeu?* Six centuries after Christine authored her *Vision*, one word, in the language of my passport: **everything**.

◊

As already admitted in the dictionary I almost stole, *jeu* is defined as **a love poem in dialogue form**. Two hundred and twenty-five pages later, the *vendicion* of Old French translates as **a sale**, *vendre* as **to sell** or **to betray**, depending on the context. *Vendage* denotes **a sale, selling**; also: **prostitution**. Two letters away, *vendenge* conveys **the vintage, vine-harvest; the wine**. To *vendengier* is **to harvest (the grape)**, and also **to pillage, plunder, destroy**. A *vendeor* is **a trader**, a *venderesse* **a woman who trades**. A *vendoise* is a bream (or similar fresh-water fish);

---

⁵³ Benjamin. "Theses on the Philosophy of History" *Illuminations*, trans. Zohn, 256.

figuratively speaking, it signifies **an object of little value: ne valoir une**. To *vendre* is **to defend, resist; assert; spend all one has; sell one's life dearly**.

◊

As the priciest English language dictionary in my university's library will attest, the word *poet* is rooted as well to *assemble, compose, fabricate,* while *translation* is kin to *carry* or *bear across*. In one of many online dictionaries populated by ads (my algorithm suggests Platinum American Express, a woman sunbathing in a yellow swimsuit), the verb *translate* is defined as *to change something into a new form.* Another entry reads: *to decide that words, behavior, or actions mean a particular thing: [example] You'll lose points if you translate too literally.* And finally: *to change writing or speech from one language into another: [infinitive] Poetry does not translate easily.*[54] Nor love.

In translating the *Jeux à Vendre* of Christine, I looked not only to the words assembled on a borrowed dictionary's pages but to the gaps between entries, the selvedge thread where one line unspools the possibility of another. Line by line, each poem composed alternatives. These, I cast parallel initial gambits, knitting dialogue with glimmer—as with the invention I almost traded for a book, not so

---

[54] https://dictionary.cambridge.org/us/dictionary/english/translate

much fabrication as stretch of the margin, not so much decorative embroidery as essential cross-stitch.

> Lepistre de othea dedie a Monsieur d'Orleans filz du Roy Charles le quint et mise en vers francoys par Xpine file de Maistre Thomas de pizan aultrement dict de bouloigne

[Inscription inside the front cover of the Duke's Manuscript, the second of Christine's assembled works, completed 1406–1408, and acquired by Jean of Barry, though likely intended for Louis d'Orleans before his murder in 1407. Paris, BnF, fr. 606.]

Christine's signature X often appears in her manuscripts, linking feminine authorship to divine authority; as she writes in *The Book of Fortune's Transformation*: "Even though my name is not well known, in order for me to be to be correctly named, just add the letters *I, N, E* to the name of the most perfect man who ever lived; no other letter is necessary."[55] If, as Spivak writes, "the task of the translator is to facilitate . . . love between the original and its shadow," Christine had just marked the spot.[56] To trace the voice in play, I looked to the crossing of the name.

---

[55] *Fortune's Transformation*, trans. Blumenfeld-Kosinski, 94.
[56] Spivak, 180.

In *The Book of the City of Ladies*, Christine tells the story of a young woman named Marina. To remain with her widowed father, who has taken holy orders, Marina dresses as a male novice and assumes the name Marinus. After the father dies, Marinus lives alone in her cell, "leading such a holy existence that . . . the monks praised her piety. None of them suspected she was, in fact, a woman."[57]

When a local inn keeper's daughter becomes pregnant and Marinus is accused of being the father, the devout maiden chooses to accept blame rather than prove her innocence by revealing her true identity. In this way,
she restores some measure of honor to the innkeeper's daughter, who gives birth to a son.

Banished from the monastery, Marinus undertakes the infant's care, feeding the child beggar's crusts. Five years pass. Still disguised as a male penitent, Marinus dies. When the monks go to wash the body, they discover, "that 'he' was in fact a woman, [and] are horrified to see the terrible wrong they had done to such a holy and innocent creature."

---

[57] *City*, III.12.1. trans. Brown-Grant, 225–227.

At Marina's burial mound, a blind man's sight is restored. The young mother who had lied out of fear and gone out of her mind is restored to her senses. "Many other miracles occurred on this site," writes Christine, "and still do today."

◊

So does surrender to Christine's text yield the name of the one who scribes at the limits of language. Poem by poem, I bind my hand with hers, Marina. Beyond the capsized boundary, we wager another telling. *Translation is the most intimate act of reading.* We enter now the fraying.

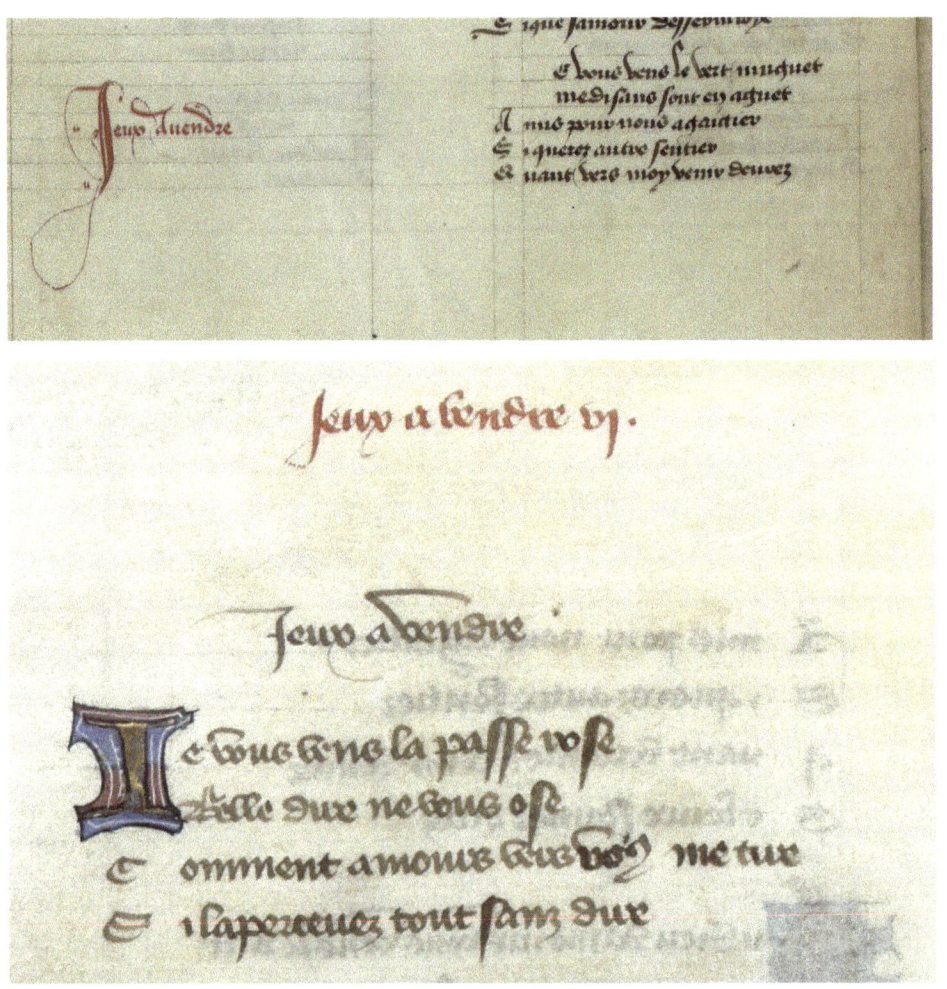

[*Jeux à vendre*, Oeuvres de « *Christine de Pizan, demoiselle* » BnF, fr. 604, fol. 36v. & *Recueil des oeuvres de « Christine de Pisan »* BnF, fr. 835, fol. 31r.]

« venditions »

1]

Je vous vens la passerose.

—Belle, dire ne vous ose

Comment Amours vers vous me tire,

Si l'apercevez tout sanz dire.

I sell to you
    A single branch of hollyhock
    —Beauty, say you dare not
    How Love towards you draws me,
    Reveals all without speaking

I sent my love
    The smallest of God's sparrows
    —Boldly, he did venture
    Love's most tempting verses
    Sweet song perched outside my window

2]

Je vous vens la fueille tremblant.

—Maint faulx amans, par leur semblant,

Font grant mençonge sembler voire,

Si ne doit on mie tout croire.

I offer for sale
    This trembling aspen leaf
    —Many false lovers, by their semblance
    Make endless lies seem truth
    So one morsel untaught is all believed

I give to you
    This vellum page unmarked
    —Love, let no deceitful pen
    Prattle gossip's tales about
    The faithful brook not the least doubt

3]
Je vous vens la paternostre.

—Vous scavez bien que je suis vostre,

Ne oncques a autre ne fus,

Si ne faittes de moy reffus,

Belle que j'aim, mais sanz demour

Me vueilliez donner vostre amour.

I offer to you

   The Lord's prayer

   —Know well that I am yours

   No other cross will I have

   Should you refuse my plea

   Beauty, whom I love, without delay

   May you be willing to give your love

I gave my love

   These wooden beads

   —Once wound about my wrist

   Another tree before us felled

   Utterly defenseless, birds

   Turned to flight. Love, no time left

   To tarry, pay quickly this destiny of words

5]

Je vous vens la fleur de mellier

—Sire joly chevalier,

Telle pour vous souvent souspire

Qui vous aime et ne l'ose dire.

I sell to you

    The best honeyed flower

    —Fine Sir, handsome rider

    Such a one is often sighed over

    Who loves and dares not a whisper

I gave my love

    A secret healing tonic

    —He, Master of gallant nights

    Wedded breathless remembrance

    Has no heart left to speak it

12]

Je vous vens la turterelle.

—Seulete et toute a par elle

Sanz per s'envole esgarée,

Ainsi suis je demourée,

Dont jamais je n'aray joye

Pour nulle chose que j'oye.

I sell to you
    This turtle dove
    —Alone and by herself apart
    Without her mate flown lost
    So cast adrift I stay
    And nevermore will I have joy
    For nothing I set store by

Fortune's thief, she sells
    My rarest mourning song
    —A single keening note
    Robs our feathered gladness
    Flees my desolate throat
    Behold remnants of plumage
    Wing scattered glass

40]

Je vous vens le blanc corbel

—Vostre gracieux corps bel

Et vostre ris savoureaux

Fait mon cuer estre amoureux

I offer for sale
    This snow-white raven
    —In great favor with your fair form
    And your delicious laughter
    Abides my loving heart entire

Lady Fortune, she did take
    The luster-bright from my curls
    —Adorned her greed-filled mannequin
    My willow-pleated robes &
    Deeded tart death my courage whole

42]

Je vous vens le dyamant.
—Sachiez que j'ay bel amant,
N'il n'est homme soubz les cieulx
A mon gré plus gracieux.

I sell to you
    This diamond rare
    —Know you well my true devotion
    Neither does any man under heaven
    Possess a more courteous station

I give to you
    This stone of blackness
    —Hold fast my fair mistress
    Under God's blue canopy I'll take
    My most desired staircase

70]

Je vous vens l'escrinet tout plein.
—Mon nom y trouverez a plain
Et de cil qu'oncques plus amay,
Par qui j'ay souffert maint esmay,
Se vous y querez proprement;
Or regardez mon se je ment.

I offer to you
   A small chest filled entirely
   —Find there my name written plainly
   And his, never more beloved
   For whom I suffered much dismay
   If you search inside properly,
   Well then, see whether I do lie

I gave my love
   The whole of my body open
   —See my signature scratched in skin
   The soul latched silent
   Forever the bitter root tasted
   One day you asked *What price, Madame?*
   Gold fleck, mint sprig, little value

'A l'enseigne de l'estoille. (Coucher à l'en. *To lye without dores all night) vnder the Canopie of the faire heauens.*

On les fait croire que les estoilles sont des papillottes. *They are made beleeue that starres be (no better then) spangles ; viz. They are extreamely gulled, or abused.*

'A midi estoille ne luit : Prov. *At mid day no starre shines ; Looke* Midi.

Estoillé : m. ée : f. *Starrie, full of starres ; poudered, or set thicke, with starres.*

Estoillée : f. *The hearbe Lyons foot, Ladies mantle, great Sanicle*

Estoiller. *To set with starres.*

Estoilleux : m. euse : f. *Starrie, full of starres, set thicke with starres.*

« *To lie without doors all night under the canopy of the fair heavens; They are made believe that stars be; At midday no starre shines; Starrie, full of stars, set thick with stars.* »

[Randle Cotgrave's *French-English Dictionary*, 1611.]

ILLUMINATED HISTORIES

> *... trouver bien et mal, bel et lait, sens et folie, et fere son preu de tout par les examples de l'estoire.*

> *... find good and evil, the beautiful and ugly, sense and folly, and profit from all through the example of history.*[58]

The unfamiliarity of words allows a certain freedom, and sometimes strange collisions. In Old French, the word *estoire* means *history*, but it's also tied to the physical object that conveys the history—the *chronicle* itself, the narrative source. *Estoire* can also mean the *story* of a factual occurrence, which is both tied to time and extends beyond it.[59]

How does our language about any one particular event shift from conveyance to legend, to a story we tell over and over again—like a star, outliving the moment of its birth?

---

[58] The *Grandes Chroniques de France*, 1.3, quoted in Hedeman, *The Royal Image*, 153.
[59] Morrison and Hedeman discuss medieval conceptions of history in *Imagining the Past in France*, 1.

As with most life-altering events, my introduction to Christine happened by accident. I was enrolled in a Chaucer course, but my attention kept wandering. One day in the library stacks, I came across a book with brief mention of Christine. Her story so compelled me, I began relearning French after an absence of thirty years so that I might get closer to her poetry.

But poetry, made of language, is not separate from the consciousness of its maker, who exists in a particular place and time in history. And so my wandering continued to unfamiliar waters. As it happens, another definition for *estoire* is *a fleet of ships*, or an *armada*. Christine lived in a time of intense historical and political upheaval, and she very intentionally wrote to effect the betterment of a court beset by vicious infighting and a king's devastating incapacity.

The illuminations depicted here, accessed through the digitized collections of the Bibliothèque nationale de France and the British Library, are from the *Chroniques* of Jean Froissart, one of the most popular vernacular histories of fourteenth-century England and France. Secular manuscripts such as Froissart's and the *Grandes chroniques de France* were typically much larger than devotional books, with lavish narrative illustrations of factual persons, battles, and spectacles. Their audiences included nobles and royals, and Christine relied upon them as an important source for her work.[60]

Charged with brilliant hues, grand pageantry, and dramatic urgency, these centuries-old illuminations relay immediate access to histories inhabited by Christine, and the possibility struck me that our eyes had gazed on the same pictorial stories. Not only the ones in the chronicles, but the ones in the sky.

Christine was the daughter of an astrologer, and I began to wonder what shape a poem might take if it were a constellation. How might it tell the story of a young queen? of an anointed king, suffering terrifying spells? of tragic entertainments? of a foreign-born noblewoman, unjustly wronged?

In close proximity to the word *estoire*, my library dictionary lists the Old French word for star: *estoile*. And if your eye wandered just a bit further, you'd find *estoile: see estoire*. Which might be translated to mean: *History is written in the stars*.

Maybe poetry is what illuminates the stories we read there.

---

[60] The influence of the *Grandes chroniques* is particularly obvious in *Vision, Fortune's Mutation*, and Christine's biography of King Charles V. Margolis, 176. Adams, 181.

[*Queen Isabeau of Bavaria.* British Library, Harley MS 4379 fol. 3r.]

« étoiles »

The queen consort enters Paris | August 1389

Nude   she stood before them   in an unknown tongue
                             her blossoming   form   avowed
                                         fit to bear   future royals
Secret pilgrimage of marriage   she was   conducted to Hymen's
                               court   where unfamiliar   kinswomen
         outfitted her in silk   flirtation   bejeweled her locks &
                whispered   clandestine wisdom   — new
        equipages   for a strange country
Three days as the Spirit rises —
                     the young King took her   hand   in gold circles
wed without dowry   & chronicled   for all   centuries how
           They spent that night together   *in great delight*
                        as you can well   *believe —*
In the time   of her   arrival
               our King exceeded   every past   ceremony
disguising his own   splendor   as she was borne high
               upon a gilded litter   weight of magnificence
           crowning her   head
A starry sky

        embroidered   with angels   & sunbeams

            canopied the Bastide   & from a *fleur-de-lys*

      fountain   honeyed wine   flowed into gold —

The procession led

          to a watchman's turret   overlooking a

             courtyard   lush with branches & foliage

where a white Hart   lay on a bed of   Justice

                   & maidens   battled

          the Lion & the Eagle with naked swords

Far above the street

       an acrobat   tricked the air

                 singing   as he

        strolled —   We watched   him balance

     lighted tapers in each hand   *(for it was now dark)*

& all who saw him wondered with marvel how it might be

[*Attack on Olivier de Clisson, Constable to King Charles VI*, rumored to have disclosed a secret love affair of the duke of Orléans. BL Harley 4379 fol. 152v.]

My mistress composes private missives for the Duke | 1391

Ardent burning   he bestowed me   a generous purse

        My lady

               quench me

How could I not?

        Six times myself   my babes' mouths

    hungry   *By my soul* —   Rumor claims

He offered   *My lady*   one thousand   gold

    crowns

        tumbled   &

From his hand   my ink   blackened

    I flame

        with desire —   Enflamed   my pen sent

Secret word to her

    My lady   countrywoman   from   beyond

    the clouded mountains : :

Duchess

        newly wed   lately wronged   *By my soul*

        My lady

               Please —

[*King Charles VI suffers an attack*. BnF, fr. 2646, fol. 153v.]

Charles VI seized by madness in the forêt of Le Mans | August 1392

Madly beloved   our King   infected by rumor   insatiable

    black bile   mounted a white steed   & led

        five thousand   men

            into a far wood —

Seeking the failed   assassin   they rode   a heat-sanded field

        scorched   air

            waved with fever

A barefoot leper   caught hold   his divine brindle   *Ride*

            no further noble King!

Fortune turns her   wheel —   High overhead

        the Noonday demon   casts   spells

Lance-clattered helmet

        bewitches   majestic sword into   loyal torsos —

            le monstre sacré   awakens

His frenzied   saddle   spurs   *Forward against the betrayers —*

    who yesterday   supped at the same   table

            born of one   womb

    the Wise King's   sons   once   brothers

They say

    the Holy   Virgin   turned her face —

[*Dance of the Wodewoses.* BL Harley MS 4380, fol. 1r.]

Bal des ardents | January 1393

Rough music — the widow's wedding entertainment
       set ablaze by the royal kinsman's torch
Flames fed by pitch & flax   linen-sewn
          burning flesh   & Devil's wildness —
Arrayed in elaborate masque   adorned by
      pleasure & forgetfulness —   our beloved King
         not fully mad   but yet aflame —
            the young azure skirt did quench
Conflagration charred to oblivion   all but he & the savage
     dancer who leapt   into the vast
Wine-dark vat —   intoxicated by sorcery's fire

[*Valentina Visconti, Duchess of Orléans*. BL Harley 4380 fol. 105r.]

Valentina   Duchess of Orléans   leaves Paris | 1396

Mother of a poet   *steadfast constant*

        she who quieted   our King's torment

            fluent in languages   exiled   by vicious

Tongues who claim her not   *ma belle soeur*

        sister of my foreign   song   but

            cursed enchantress   wicked intruder

Round with child   she poisons

        her own blood —   the gossip-

            bitter apple   rolls upon

        the nursery   floor

She who bore   eight lives — pledged four to God —

        sheltered   the fruit   of another womb

Motherless mother   she tended

        all trees — one grew strong

He who rode alongside the Maid

        avenged   our faith   & her slandered

            heart   now buried   alongside

The porcupine's   quill   —   does yet sting

My mistress   felled by illness   walks along the River Seine | 1400

In dream   she hears the late king's   clocks sound

      the hours   & the church bells

Rouse   her   stricken limbs — Awake

     before the sun

              before her children

Rise   she lifts the latch   steals into

     the dark morning

              after the last carousing

Heads toward the water's edge   *au bord du fleuve*

     dreams she might   slip in —

          My mistress   infected by loss

              prisoner of grief   deaf to God —

     at the lobe of her ear   neither clock   nor bells

         nor   angel's whisper

     but the aged tongue   of the forever   mortal sibyl

Gather now   *the shards*

     from your father's treasure

              remember how

     your beloved   did teach you this hand —

         I vow I will   never forsake you

Wake now   do not let the green river take you

                                          but write instead

            your vision —

                    The door to all our misfortunes was opened

                      & I   who was still very

young   entered —

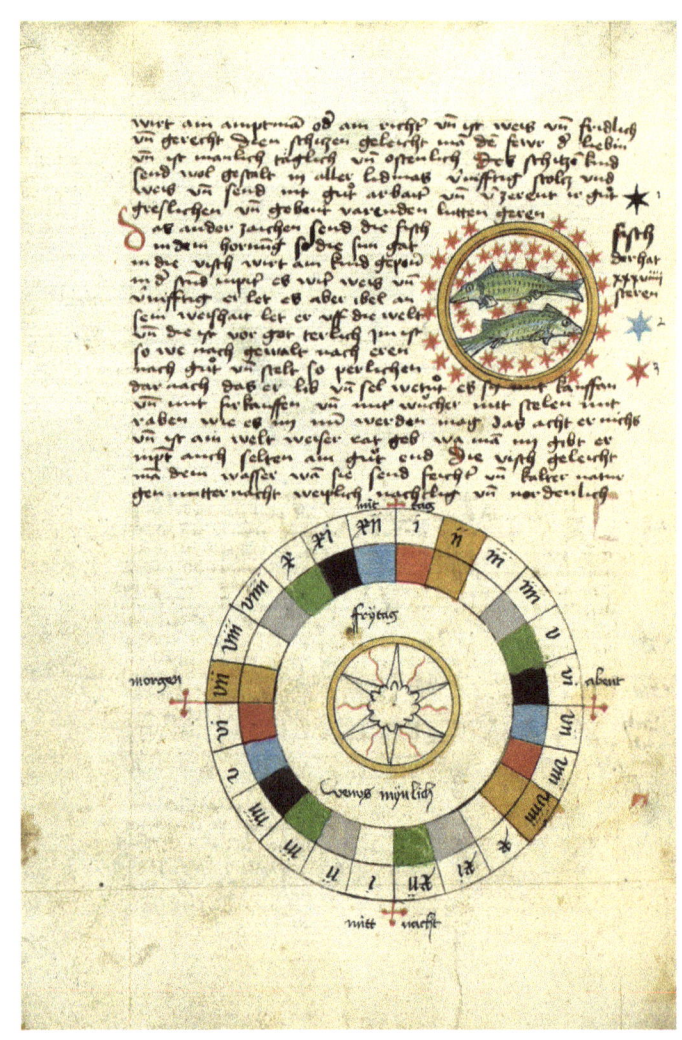

[« Pisces; Diagram for Friday » *Astronomical Miscellany* c.1464. MS. Ludwig XII 8, fol. 56v., Getty Museum.]

[I was born   the stars of two fish]

That's what Mistress says   & her father foretold my

arrival   so it must be so

She says this is how I swim across paper

      ink flow into ocean   How is it possible

to remember the morning of one's own baptism?   Since that vessel did

bring me to this land   separate from the sea

      my body has not been immersed

but there courses   a river through the village   & if you walk there

when the water is deep & still   you can see   ribbons of fish

      tiny   nibs   trailing golden pigment —

My mistress tells first   how her spirit was transported | 1403

Begins the pilgrimage   of strange countries   alps   meadows   forests
           rivers
                  It seemed to me my spirit left my body

Along the half-finished journey   she inscribed   how two serpents
           entwined   the blind seer —

As prayers   on the altar   change a daughter
           my mistress

Once married   young-widowed   became a master

The hours of my mistress are long but not inconsolable | October 1425

Birdsong   bells
the rooster calls   &

the moon   foolish from carousing
her path   across the night

slips into the earth

— • —

Before
the canopied route

      a stand of trees
      at attention
            to sunlight

— • —

Morning grass
      oceans the field
      apple-sweet
ripening
      vermillion

— • —

Swans lift off the water
   &   their feathers
cloud   the sky
       disappeared
in the rain-frothed river

— • —

Wind through the aspens

      each day
a little of their green flies away

   uncovering
   globes in the branches

readying
the forest for sleep

— • —

Days turn
to years

each night closer
     to her beloved

lit with stars she can bear it

— • —

Where stone
            bridges
the river
no time passes   only a boat

blue   flat
over lily roots

— • —

As when   from a far distance

you see another   ❧

whether   walking towards
               or away

you cannot tell

BOOK II
OF COUNTRIES [FAMILIAR & STRANGE]

[*The Beautiful Things That Christine Saw in the Firmament Under the Guidance of the Sibyl.* BL Harley 4431, fol. 189v.]

TO DREAM THE IMPOSSIBLE REAL: CHRISTINE'S « PATH » AS CASE STUDY IN MEDIEVAL DREAM POETRY

I. Prologue: Before & After the Dream

Dreams teach us. Our dreams are the greatest poets.[61]

On the last day of March, 1403, a poem of some 6,400 lines was presented to the duke of Berry in his Paris residence. Two additional copies were given to the dukes of Burgundy and Orléans, and while the manuscript is dedicated to the king himself, "illustrious in honor, exalted in dignity . . . most worthy lily of magnificent splendor . . . ,"[62] King Charles VI had, by now, been stricken with the incapacitating mental illness that threatened his reason and his reign. The name of the woman who composed the poem is not spoken within its text until line 6329, but she was known to each of the dukes, each maneuvering for power in an ailing kingdom.

---

[61] Cixous, "The School of Dreams" in *Three Steps on the Ladder of Writing*, trans. Sellars, 71.

[62] *The Path of Long Study* in *The Selected Writings of Christine de Pizan*, trans. Brownlee, 59–87.

The poem relayed a dream the woman had on the night of October 5, 1402, a dream in which she travels to the far ends of the earth and the firmament above; a dream in which she comes not face to face with God, but with others who have—others real and imagined who have served as teachers in the books the woman has read. In this dream, the woman is not only voyager but witness to a celestial dispute, charged to transmit a worthy account to the French court, so that it might render wise judgment to remedy human-made destruction.

The poem's dedication asks these real-world men of power to excuse the woman's "simplemindedness" and "mistakes through ignorance," imploring "Powerful princes, do not despise my little poem because I am worth little." Nevertheless, in the manuscript she at once imagines, authors, transcribes, and messengers, its maker ventures not only to realize the seemingly impossible, she undertakes to instruct a king.

II. Here Is Introduced the Dreamer & the Nature of Her Dream That Is Also a Book

> *No, the dreamer-sleeper (at the heart of sleep, in its profound center, inaccessible, insensible) is not prey to the grief that presses heavily on all the living, neither is [s]he simply resting; [s]he is busy inventing h[er] life.*[63]

---

[63] Risset, *Sleep's Powers*, trans. Moxley, 41.

Born in Venice in 1364 and brought to France as a young child after her father accepted a position as royal physician and astrologer in the court of King Charles V, Christine de Pizan has been widowed thirteen years when we meet her at the poem's beginning, neither dreaming nor sleeping, but grieving anew the untimely death of her husband. His loss, and those of her father and King Charles the Wise, left Christine responsible for the care of her three small children, mother, and a niece in a country beset by internal and external strife. She was just twenty-five and easily might have remarried. Instead, she decided to earn a living through writing.

Alone now in her study, Christine reveals to the reader the full force of her despair, blaming Fortune for depriving her of a past happy life and for imprisoning her heart "in such tight bonds that it is weary of struggling." And yet this heart is not so weary that that woman in whom it beats does not take up her pen to write the book that becomes the book we are reading, the *Le Livre du chemin de long estude* [*The Book of the Path of Long Study*].[64] In this regard, Christine's *Chemin* works exactly as other dream poems of the time period: as a literary construction,

---

[64] For a complete translation of the Harley 4431 manuscript into modern French, see Tarnowski's *Le chemin de longue étude*. An English version of Tarnowski's introduction is found in Altmann, 181–97. In its use of *Chemin* to designate Christine's poem, this essay follows Tarnowski's example.

making its reader aware, "that it has a beginning and an end . . . ; that it has a narrator, whose experience constitutes the subject-matter . . . ; that its status is that of an imaginative fiction . . . ; in short that it is not a work of nature but a work of art."[65]

It is as a made thing, too, that distinguishes the medieval dream poem from mystical literature, sometimes called the *dream vision*. As Helen Philips notes: "Most dream poems are consciously literary. . . . Dream poems make the worlds inside and outside the dream frame seem significantly distinct. Mystical visions, in contrast, are presented as a direct knowledge of God's truth, the divine reality suddenly present within everyday, waking reality, and breaking any distinction between them."[66]

In the *Chemin*, as with other medieval dream poems—Chaucer's *Parliment of the Fowls* or Jean de Meun's reworking of Guillaume de Lorris's *Le Roman de la Rose*, for example—the dream as it is recounted may include startling imagery, divine beings, or seemingly visionary truths, but these always occur as part of the dream narrative and never does that story claim to write itself. What "the fictional device of the dream" *does* facilitate is a multiplicity of literary techniques, subject matter,

---

[65] Spearing, *Medieval Dream-Poetry*, 4.
[66] Philips and Havely, *Chaucer's Dream Poetry*, 7.

and places of slippage whereby a reader might enter as if she, too, were a dreamer, crossing a threshold from one realm of consciousness to another. If ever there existed a literature of intertextuality, of entering into existing texts as a method both of response and of creation, it would be the medieval dream poem.

III. Here Is Explored the High Regard for the Learned Who Came Before

> *When we speak of the Middle Ages as the ages of authority we are usually thinking about the authority of the Church. But they were the age not only of her authority, but of authorities. If their culture is regarded as a response to environment, then the elements in that environment to which it responded most vigorously were manuscripts. Every writer, if he possibly can, bases himself on an earlier —writer, follows an auctour.*[67]

As expected, Christine will indeed embark on a voyage, but just as the planets were thought to transmit certain influences, so, too, will the narrative of this dreamer be affected by bedtime reading matter. Still very much awake and looking

---

[67] Lewis, *The Discarded Image*, 5.

to assuage her despair, the book Christine selects is Boethius's *Consolation of Philosophy*.

Written in the sixth century and acknowledged by C.S. Lewis as "one of the most influential books ever written in Latin," the *Consolation* combines prose and poetry, Greek philosophy and Christian faith, as it recounts Boethius's dream-time encounter with Lady Philosophy while he awaits death for treason. Before falling out of favor with Roman Emperor Theodoric, Boethius had served as a high ranking government official, and Lewis maintains that "the consolation Boethius seeks is not for death but for ruin," that which Lady Fortune wreaks at whim.[68] The only constructive response to such capriciousness—which is to say, the contingency of life—arrives in those truths revealed through the conversation Lady Philosophy has with the imprisoned Boethius, many of which Christine relays in the *Chemin*: "Happiness can only result from a goodness which cannot fail. . . . How . . . can the clarity that illumines enlighten you if you remain dark, having in you none of your own brightness?"[69] In the double-consciousness

---

[68] Lewis, 75–77.

[69] The section of *The Consolation* to which Christine refers is found in Book 3.met.10, quoted here from Goins and Wyman, 94-95:
>   Come here and be freed,
>   chained captives of earth
>   caught in desire-bound minds....

encompassed by the dream poem, in the darkness that sleep brings, such brightness might be found.

Along with these glimmerings, the *Consolation* offers suitable gravitas for the darkening thoughts of an autumn evening,[70] and in reaching for Boethius, Christine allies herself, too, with a particular gravitas of authority. If, as Christine claims of her choice, a "good example is very helpful in achieving comfort and removing displeasure," this particular example also lends credence to Christine's account, confirming her as a worthy teller, as it points the reader to the kind of *auctours* that may be encountered in the narrative to come—venerated ancestors human, imagined, and allegorical. True to "the characteristically medieval type of imagination" of the writers of her time, Christine's imaginings in the *Chemin* are not "a transforming imagination like Wordsworth's or a penetrative imagination

> Neither Tagus nor Hermus
> offering ripe golden sands,
> nor hot-flowing Indus,
> brewing its jewels,
> sparkling, gleaming, clear and green—
> can illuminate the vision
> of man's darkened mind.

[70] Phillips confirms the literary intentionality implicit in such decisions: "Analysis of dream poems reveals that their use of frames and the first-person narrator are rarely merely conventional or perfunctory. *The Roman de la rose* had firmly established the seasonal opening as virtually a standard part of the dream poem but later poets seem to calculate carefully the different effects of a winter, spring or harvest reference." From "Dream Poems," 378.

like Shakespeare's. [Hers] is a realizing imagination."[71] Even as the author of her own experience, Christine respected the accepted role of narrator-dreamer as one who composes within an well-regarded lineage and does not venture out alone.

IV. How Out of Old Books New Ideas Are Found

> *O glory and light of other poets, let the long study and the great love that has made me search thy volume avail me.*

These are the words a relieved Dante, lost in the middle of the journey, exclaims to Virgil after he appears to help the lone pilgrim upon his arduous path.[72] Christine relays his invocation, almost word for word, when her dream-self declares she " . . . would use [it] instead of the Gospel or the sign of the Cross when I encountered various dangers and perils." That Christine avails herself of Dante's model as both author and protagonist of the *Chemin* is perhaps no surprise: The *Commedia* was written in Christine's native Italian, and while she was certainly fluent in French and adopted it as the language in which she composed, she makes explicit note of Dante's words "to describe what Virgil had taught: how to compose in the beautiful style."[73]

---

[71] Lewis, 206.

[72] The lines from Dante's *Inferno* (trans. Sinclair) are found in Canto I.82–84.

[73] Blumenfeld-Kosinski, 74. Margolis also notes Dante's *Divine Comedy*, particularly the *Inferno*, as "the first obvious example of Dante's influence in French literature." *An Introduction*, 96. Additionally, Tarnowski credits Christine as the "second author in France, after Philippe de Mézières" to speak of Dante, "but she was the first to make use of the *Inferno* as a model for her own work." *Le Chemin*, 155n.3, my translation.

Christine is believed to have had at least some knowledge of Latin, but as revolutionary as Dante's vernacular was for the late-medieval literary world, the effect of an unmediated reading experience must have felt an unprecedented freedom. The status of Christine's father and of her husband (a court notary) had opened unique access to the extensive library of Charles V, but the serious knowledge acquired by Christine came about primarily after their deaths as she embarked on a rigorous decade-long program of self-study. While never a mystic, Christine maintained an active religious faith, and to rely on the words of a poet over those of the Church speaks to the depth of trust she must have felt for their teaching.

As for the figure selected to guide the *Chemin*'s pilgrim on her path—the Cumaean sibyl—she, too, has a direct line to Dante; after all, who could be more fitting than the one who led Virgil's hero, Aeneas, through the frightening caves of the Underworld?[74] Christine names her Almethea, the one who prophesies, too, in Virgil's *Eclogue*s. Phillips notes that "authoritative dream guides go back to classical

---

[74] In her extensive biography of Christine, Charity Cannon Willard surmises: "It has been supposed that Christine could not have known the *Aeneid* directly, even though she quotes some verses from it in *The Book of Peace*, but she could have known some copies of this text which were produced in Paris workshops during the early years of the fifteenth century." Willard also details the opinion that Christine knew, "in any case, Boccaccio's *De claris mulieribus*, a principal source for *The Book of the City of Ladies*, as well as the *Moralized Ovid*, both of which retell the story of the sibyl Almethea." *Life and Works*, 101, 231n.35.

dream narratives such as Cicero's *Somnium Scipionis* (c.55 BCE), and may arrive in the guise of deity, human or a personification."[75] In the *Chemin*, the sibyl appears as

> a lady of great stature, with a very virtuous and wise appearance, and a dignified manner. She was neither young nor pretty, but aged and very calm. She did not wear a crown, for she was no crowned queen; rather, she was simply coiffed with a veil tied around her head, and she wore, according to the old-fashioned manner, a wide tunic. She gave the impression of strength and durability. This lady seemed to me to be an honorable, calm, temperate, and very wise woman—the mistress of all her powers.[76]

This is not how the sibyl is portrayed by another poet of Christine's certain acquaintance, Ovid. Neither does Christine ask for Ovid's assistance on the path, though he certainly makes an appearance. For her spurning of the sun god Phoebus Apollo, Ovid's sibyl must age until she is reduced to an ampulla prison, but Christine restores full body, voice, and prophetic power to the one who will guide her. It is perhaps a daring move, reversing a fate reported by Ovid and placing an aged human woman in the exalted position of *auctour*, but Christine also knew well that to receive even a morally worthy male companion in a dream

---

[75] Phillips, "Dream Poems," 377.
[76] Blumenfeld-Kosinski, 66.

would be to compromise her reputation as a woman of virtue. Christine's dreamer might not "possess enough knowledge for [her] understanding to be worthy" of the Sibyl's guidance, but Christine the writer understood fully the implications of her chosen teacher.

V. Between Earth & Heaven, the Dream Occurs

> *[Poetic reverie] is a reverie which poetry puts on the right track, the track an expanding consciousness follows. This reverie is written, or, at least, promises to be written. It is already facing the great universe of the blank page. . . . Poetic reverie gives us the world of worlds. Poetic reverie is a cosmic reverie.*[77]

> *I was amazed at these wonders, but nevertheless I kept turning my eyes back to earth.*[78]

The Sibyl appears at a crucial time in the text: after Christine has found personal consolation for her grief through reading Boethius, but before the narrative of the

---

[77] Bachelard, *The Poetics of Reverie*, trans. Russell, 13.
[78] Macrobius, *Commentary on the Dream of Scipio*, trans. Stahl, 74.

dream proper begins. Between waking and sleeping, a liminal space opens whereby might be entered a world made possible by dream. But, on the edge of sleep, before this world can be experienced, the reality of the world *as it is* enters Christine's consciousness—and that world is so filled with discord, strife, and chaos, that to imagine it otherwise seems itself an impossible dream. It is between these two states—impossible and possible, real and imagined, waking and sleeping—that the journey of the *Chemin* will occur. Such does Christine's depiction remain in keeping with other dream poems of the Middle Ages as described by Steven F. Kruger: "associated with both earth and heaven. . . . Navigating a course between upward-and downward-looking visions, the middle vision offers a way of exploring the connections between the world in which we find ourselves and the transcendent realm for which we yearn."[79]

Such does the Sibyl arrive at exactly that point where Christine's desire for the "peace, joy, concord, and love" found in heaven exceeds her ability to create them on earth. But it is *because* of that desire—and the diligence already demonstrated—that the Sibyl believes Christine worthy: In this sense, dreamer and guide choose each other—one earthly, one equipped to ascend the firmament.

For all the far reaches of their travels, Christine never abandons hold of her own place. When they catch sight of the nine muses bathing in the Fountain of Wisdom, Christine neither approaches the muses nor asks for a sip from the

---

[79] Kruger, *Dreaming in the Middle Ages*, 130.

fountain, as did those male philosophers and poets who "in times past . . . . when they wanted to slake their thirst in the sweet water that kept them wise." Nor do the venerated men appear on the page, as they do in Dante's Elysian Fields; only their names are brought into existence through the Sibyl's voice. And while Christine's own father is among this illustrious enumeration, the Sibyl reminds the beloved daughter that she "cannot be part of this noble school," as was Dante.

Neither, however, is Christine made to enter the "dark and obscure" path that leads "to hell with no hope of return." Her path is the one called Long Study, ". . . reserved for those of noble heart and subtle mind."

VI. The Dreamer As Scribe

> *They tell me their stories in their language, in the twilight, all alike or almost, half gentle half cruel, before any day, any hour. I don't wake, the dream wakes me with one hand. . . . Docile I say not a word. The dream dictates. I obey eyes closed. . . . The dream commands. I do.*[80]

---

[80] Cixous, *Dream I Tell You*, trans. Bie Brahic, 1.

When the path leads beyond the terrestrial realm, the Sibyl calls upon *Imagination*, which releases a ladder made out of a material "called *speculation*, beloved by all subtle intelligences." With the Sibyl's help, Christine begins her ascent—not as far as Dante scaled the Golden Ladder, nor as far as Jacob to hear God's voice, but as far as the fifth heaven, "beautiful, clear shining and most exalted." That Christine's method of entry is a ladder-that-mirrors reflects a common trope in dream poetry,[81] and makes sense in the *Chemin*, not only as a method of extending knowledge beyond the self, but as a signal to the self-reflexive act the genre performs, "examining its own constructs and movement." As articulated by Kruger, "the self-conscious dream poem is not independent of the external reality or truth that it attempts to represent. The dream poem's self-reflexivity, in other words, often leads it into questions of epistemology."[82] Such questions of knowledge and truth, value and virtue, are exactly what occupy the last section of the *Chemin*, as Christine assumes the role of silent listener and scribe for the allegorical debate waged by Ladies Reason, Wealth, Nobility, Chivalry, and Wisdom.

---

[81] Kruger provides a detailed discussion regarding mirrors as a traditional image for spiritual ascent, wisdom, or truth, including Dante's depiction in the *Paradiso* : "Set thy mind behind thine eyes and make of them mirrors to the shape which in this mirror will appear to thee." (21.15–17)
[82] Krueger, 136

Keeping in mind that the words of these noble figures do in fact spring from the same brain that guides Christine's pen, the debate recounted is intended neither as showy display nor star-shot philosophical exercise: as she notes in the *Chemin*'s Prologue, Christine intends the message she delivers to help King Charles VI "render a judgment" that will help resolve the many crises threatening the kingdom. In extending the dream poem's multiplicity to include a mirror for princes, the *Chemin* itself becomes a mirror of the right path, whereby all the knowledge and learning displayed—literary, historical, geographical, astronomical—lead to a genuine goal: the betterment of the world. As Andrea Tarnowski notes, "Like her predecessor Boethius, [Christine] feels compelled to find another, greater, more lasting meaning in what goes on around her; whether as a traveling protagonist in the *Chemin* or a developing author, Christine is a perpetual pilgrim, an idealist and moralist with her sights set beyond the visible."[83]

And yet those sights, however impossible, always return to the real. Maybe this is part of their impossibility, and yet, in the very fact of the *Chemin's* existence as a written text, Christine does achieve it: She dreams the impossible real. Within the dream, she imagines the music of celestial movement and then writes it into a book so that we can turn the pages in our hands. Like Dante glancing earthward

---

[83] Tarnowski, *A Casebook*, 187.

or the heavenly traveler reported in *Scipio's Dream*,[84] so too does Christine look down to see what "seemed to me (I assure you) . . . the entire earth as a little sphere, as round as a ball." She might not ascend as high as the Empyrean Sphere, but neither will she fall "like Icarus," for, as the Sibyl points out, "it is not presumption that leads [Christine] into this exalted region, rather [a] great desire to see beautiful things that impels." Such has been the dream of poets since the first dreams written down.

VII. The Dream Made Real

> *Dreams pave the way for life, and they determine you without you understanding their language. One would like to learn this language, but who can teach and learn it? Scholarliness alone is not enough; there is knowledge of the heart that gives deeper insight. The knowledge of the heart is in no book and is not to be found in the mouth of any teacher, but grows out of you like the green seed from the dark earth...*[85]

---

[84] Brownlee contends that "For the Middle Ages, the single most important instance of a heavenly traveler looking back toward earth was Cicero's *Scipio's Dream*, read along with Macrobius's famous *Commentary* (81n.2). The importance of Macrobius to the Medieval world is confirmed by Lewis in *The Discarded Image*, 60–69.
[85] Jung, *The Red Book*, 233.

A case study is a single example of many, but in the case of the *Chemin*, it is also singular, meaning at once representative and wholly exceptional. Its author took as her example those who came before—their methods, their figures, their images, sometimes even their very words. Those of Dante she read in the language of her birth. Those of Boethius solaced her to dream. But Christine was the one who placed herself in the text. Though not physically imprisoned as was Boethius, nor exiled as was Dante, Christine nevertheless worked within the confines of restriction. Some of these she broke by writing publicly as a woman. Others she broke simply through diligent study of what the men wrote, and of how they wrote it. As Lewis notes, "At his most characteristic, medieval man was not a dreamer nor a wanderer. He was an organiser, a codifier, a builder of systems."[86] So, too, was Christine a wholehearted believer of a "single, complex, harmonious Model of the Universe." In recreating the inner workings of their common cosmology, she looked to exemplar magicians and adopted their very best tricks. The *Chemin* is a record of that learning. The singular thing she did was to accomplish it.

---

[86] Lewis, 10.

VIII. Epilogue: It Is Finished, But It Is Not the End

> *From everywhere, images invade the air, go from one world to another, and call both ears and eyes to enlarged dreams. Poets abound, the great and the small, the famous and the obscure, those who love and those who dazzle. Whoever lives for poetry must read everything. When one allows himself to be animated by new images, he discovers iridescence in the images of old books. Poetic ages unite in a living memory. The new age awakens the old. The old age comes to live again in the new.*[87]

The poem ends abruptly with a sharp knock into the domestic everyday realm, Christine's mother awakening her late-sleeping daughter. No matter how grand her dreams, a woman of 1402 did not easily realize her imaginings into existence. Even in the fifth heaven, Christine knew her place, but it didn't keep her from taking a seat at her desk, writing as the *auctours* had. It didn't stop her from reading their manuscripts, creating her own, and writing in this one that her "name will be resplendent long after [her] death." She doesn't (yet) claim this herself: it's prophesied by the Almethea on the October night of her dream.

---

[87] Bachelard, trans. Russell, 25.

We cannot know for certain how *The Book of the Path of Long Study* was received by its royal recipients, or even if it was read. Clearly, it did not intervene in the events of history—by 1420, those particular dukes of Berry, Burgundy, and Orléans will all be dead, the French kingdom shattered by war, the ordered workings of the cosmos on their way to nostalgic renderings.

But five hundred years later after its initial dreaming—almost to the month—a poet named Rilke will place Christine's name in a book, and her *Chemin* in a king's hands. Through the glass case of his madness, Rilke's king will be moved by the dream he reads, but it won't be the surety of its transcription nor the earnestness of its debate. As with Boethius, as with Dante, the mechanism of resonance will be the dreamer's singular humanness, broken and enduring though a seemingly impossible real:

> On such days the king was filled with benign awareness. Had a painter of that time been seeking some indication for existence in Paradise, he could have found no more perfect model than the assuaged figure of the king, as it stood at one of the high windows in the Louvre under the droop of its shoulders. He was turning the pages of the little book by Christine de Pisan [sic] which is

called 'The Way of Long Learning' and was dedicated to him. He was not reading the erudite polemics of that allegorical parliament which had undertaken to discover the prince who should be worthy to rule over the whole earth. The book always opened for him at the simplest passages: where it spoke of the heart which for thirteen long years, like a retort over the fire of suffering, had only served to distil the water of bitterness for the eyes; he understood that true consolation only began when happiness was long enough gone and over forever. Nothing was more precious to him than this comfort. And while his gaze seemed to embrace the bridge beyond, he loved to see the world through this heart moved to great ways by the powerful Cumaean,—the world of those days: the adventurous seas, the strange-towered cities held shut by the pressure of distances, the ecstatic loneliness of the assembled mountains, and the heavens, explored in fearsome doubt, which were only now closing like an infant's skull.[88]

---

[88] Rilke, *The Notebooks of Malte Laurids Brigge*, trans. Herter Norton, 185.

[*Mappemondes* from the *Chroniques de Saint-Denis* with signature of King Charles V, 1310-1320. Sainte-Geneviève, Paris MS 782 fol. 374v.]

« rêves »

In the holy town of stained glass

Everything is made of five colors —   silica   sand   cobalt   copper
    ash.   The barns are metallic   with oxidated   animals
cut from a red-hot iron.   Here   you have a man   with a sword

in his mouth   you have a horn   with stars   you have
    monsters.   You have a beggar   scribing prophesies
under watch   of a sacred cow.   The blue of the sky no longer exists.

Inside the transept rose   the queen of heaven sits   her halo
silvered yellow   the folds of her gown   applied with a fine
    brush dipped in iron   diluted with vinegar   fixed with fire.

Weightless   she reigns   radiating spokes.   Opposite the
    apocalypse   the passion.   In the right spandrel   of the arch
angels   hold the instruments   this one holds the nails.

Barefoot & dressed as a penitent   a king ransoms a crown
    from the grasp   of an emperor.   It is said   an oath
pledged   in the presence of thorns   promises a miracle.

In the country of prehistory

a tree flames tulips   to celebrate the revolution.   There are Paleolithic churches   monoliths   underground refuges marked on the legend.   Persimmon lanterns glow from limestone quarries.

At the turnabout   along the railroad tracks   you will be asked   to cede the passage   seed the conifer   &   if you walk opposite the gravestones you will cross a path melded with autumn.

Before the intersection   *toutes directions*   is posted a sign of a village in flower   its main street   leading to a grotto   stacked with three virgins   Saint Marc with his lion   a basin in the head of a camel.

After a long journey   they thirst   radiating on foot   carrying curatives   making their pilgrimage.   The camel dips his mouth to the source   *the waters being supposed to remedy the problems of sight*.   In the twilight   between the dog & the wolf it might be centuries.

In the center of her chest   a carnation flares

crimson   at the sill.   Souvenir wrappings   clementine peel
map of veins   tracing the city.   Each color

travels a name.   Winter hours   underground
we hear bells.   Along the marine river   she serenades
lament without shelter.   Palm over palm   we

ride through trilled walls   disembark at vacated castles.
In another century   a mathematician   jettisoned   coins
from the butcher's tower   to prove emptiness.

In another century   pilgrims flowed   on tributaries.

What if you were   to leave your children   in the care
of your beautiful neighbor   calculate the tax with   a lantern
gear   teeth   parallel the axle?   At every turn of the wheel

the birds would alight their cage.

In the chapel of invention

the watchmaker   maps   constellations   eleven concentric
whorls   contain an amulet   of flowers

medallions   inlaid with crystals   a cup   adorned with pinholes &
set atop a plinth   two interlocking   amphorae
with an ovum above

silent turning

the soul enters the body   by way of   a star
its intricate form   carved from a single   block of firmament
lathe-centered prayer

spindles the architecture   haloing circles

we watch   miniature orbits   transfixed by music
turned in wood   turned in ivory   turned   in secret
three witnesses vouch

the compass   is not separate from the chiming

In the station of the grand line

the wars ran   a departure   of infantrymen   between
        destinations   four rivers   sculpted in stone   two women
tend direction east wields a sword & shield   west   a key & scepter

at the crossing of roads   a star-fort citadel   nominative   locative
        terminus of   kilometer zero   all roads lead to
attrition   the baptism of princes celebrated   with sugared almonds

between battles   a child   tucks his form
        underneath the Deco staircase   where each passenger walks
a penny flattens   on the track   iron wears the face —

from the platform   the soldier waves   &   somewhere
        in the middle of the country   a man digs an ocean   into a field
a deer scratches messages   into a tree

In the middle of Paris   you will find a fig tree

not far from where the children were taken.   It grows as it always has
unpruned wild   boughs parallel the ground   small hands almost
reaching.   Saturday afternoon   we enter the gates   in search of

rest   a bench offers itself   we sit.   From your great coat pocket
you pull water   as if from a well   we drink.   The garden vibrates

with families   tired from the day   not yet finished.   Each
mother holds a hand   each father lets one go   racing ahead
as if it were summer   tree green   fruit sweetening to purple.   Earlier

you walked me to the square   where every side   is like another
in a place like that   you cannot know   where you are   where
you are   headed.   Here   in the garden   we eat pecans

imported from another land.   You paid the shopkeeper   we walked
through the door.   We walked here   through Saturday streets
thronged   wove through gates   as if there were   no   east no

west no south   every direction   pointing to   this tree
no plaque on the wall   as if it were
the autumn before   the train departed   &   every child returned.

In the medieval kingdom   the keys

        open sunlight   through the mechanism   of a sliding door   You enter stone   by way of   an octagonal   tower   fortified   ramparts   pepperbox   roof

      Outside   the disappeared church   an arrow-tree river marks the old moat ditch   Down   the holy ghost   cellar   pilgrims   & paupers   shelter   the crusaded rose

     You can taste   a conquest of petals   crushed   into history   tonic beauty   candied balm   The   apothecary   distills syrup   from   a coat of arms

     Find the mason   the stonecutter   quarryman money-changer   Full the cloth   tax the harvest   rent the tithe   barn   Watch all the   storied   goods rip apart

     Vaulted parapet   watchtower prison   capitals adorned with foliage   On the crossroads map   a spotted dog   darts out   a graffitied cave   along the route   that seeks   travelers

Inside the salle de fêtes

room of holidays   stanza of little surprises   all the windows fly
into open   wind-laced tangle   green shutters   over iron

she regards   an arcade of marvels   rings exchanged
kingdoms acquired   every portal   a new violence —

flèche of the lance   crack in the heel   in case of accident   fire
evacuation   a cavalry on the talus   replaces the crucifixion

behind the former station   now the village

take   the pavement of the soprano   to the blue aster
planet in a flower   wakeful night   fitful sleep

at the point   where the bridge meets the birds
a house with watchtowers   numbered second

sentries keep   their guard   furiosity   along the *chemin des sages*

In the cathedral city   when it rains

you see the stone of the church   become violet   you see
    stone turn to spirit   you understand   the miter as organism
& the columns   as able to make   music   it's like

a big boat for everyone   & this boat is sailing   to the holy
    land   where mountain   becomes prayer   & crystal
feldspar   flecked with gold   & you can find your way

out of the blackest forest   along the boulevard   of human rights
    the train speeds along   the canal   along   the rim
of the world   pharmacy of the angel   time as spectacle   time

as geological   the cycle *solaire*   you pass   a construction
    of curved glass   tent shelters   the tiniest   of pale
blue eggs   there is a house   an emperor built for his wife —

beyond paper regiments   beyond   the school of English
    keep going   you will see an iris in a tree   keep walking
this is only the beginning   to enter   is to know paradise

[*Histoire ancienne jusqu'à César.* MS. Ludwig XIII fol. 1r., J. Paul Getty Museum, c.1390.]

IN THE COUNTRY OF CHRISTINE

> *Not everyone is given access to this other world where the dead and the dying live. We are not all guests of the dead, this wisest of companies. If we can't get there by dying, then let's go there by dreaming.*[89]

Apples fall from tree branches, and colliding stars vibrate through light years. Such do gravitational forces magnify quotidian wonders. How best for earthbound travelers to cross curvatures of time and space? I once ventured to a medieval city to trace another poet's journey and happened upon the strangest of ordinary creatures wandering the banks of its rivers.

Dreamer as traveler, a notion transported inside language, *rêve*—French word for *dream*—wandering easily into *river*, carrying passengers across to unknown countries, no ticket for the ferryman.

Another way to dream in French is *songer*: to think about, to envisage, to muse, contemplate, wonder. Drifting between two shores of dream language, *songer*

---

[89] Cixous, *Three Steps on the Ladder of Writing*, trans. Sellars, 59. Additional quotations throughout.

conveys more lyrical freight, a verb linked to a possible future, not to sleep—though *rêver* might also stray into vision, daydream, imagined desire. As a noun, *un rêve* can also verge into nightmare, where *un songe* never does.

In mid-twentieth century Paris, a collective of artists, writers, and visionary imaginers set out on foot to remap individual experience of urban landscape through unplanned encounters. As defined by Situational theorist Guy Debord, the *dérive*—French for *drift*—is a practice in which "one or more persons during a certain period drop their relations, their work and leisure activities, and all their other usual motives for movement and action, and let themselves be drawn by the attractions of the terrain and the encounters they find there."[90]

Drifting as a means of upending habit, of bypassing usual routes in resistance to becoming a tourist in the existing cartography. The dreamer resists sleepwalking, the kind of somnolence that falls into death. How to cross the curvature between the known and the strange? How not to topple into the gap between tourism and waking dream?

Go toward foreign lands, toward the foreigner in ourselves. Traveling in the unconscious, that inner foreign country, foreign country, foreign home, country of lost countries.

*

---

[90] Guy Debord, "Theory of the Dérive," trans. Ken Knabb.

For a brief time, I lived in the small French city of Tours, not so far from where Jeanne d'Arc raised the siege at Orléans. You can see signs of the Maid's passage along the River Loire, dividing line of the warring factions that drove Christine from Paris and into sanctuary in 1418. One morning along the south bank of the Loire, I saw a man walking a goat on a leash. The goat wore a hat, as if to disguise its small horns. We all three of us meandered along.

Back towards the city center and bewildered by narrow, unfamiliar streets, I left all my crossings to the chance of signals. If one light flashed green before another, that's the route I took. The strategy wasn't compelled by rebellion so much as blind trust, but it did allow a particular orientation over a long-standing, ever-evolving map. The oldest quarter of the city, called *le Vieux Tours*, dates to the Middle Ages. One friend resided there in a building of half-timbered framing and plaster. It stands a few blocks west of the municipal library, built along the Loire in 1957 and closed for renovation the summer of my wanderings.

My friend who lived in the medieval construction spoke little English, and I, little French. Still, we managed a conveyance of understanding, lifting each other into new words, enunciations, and nuances. *Songe* is one form of dreaming, and in English *une songerie* translates to *reverie*: a waking dream, a delirium, a losing into thought. Maybe closer to *rêve*, *reverie* tumbles into river, coursing us to a long-departed world known only by the remnants of a city plan. Such sites might still be visited via aircraft. Or a dreamer might wander the heights of a shuttered library staircase to gaze over the current of another time and place. She might look out the window-seat of a book and spot the mode of transport—a wooden boat, its name illuminated on the bow: *Yes, words really do dream.*

*

Tour : m. *A turne, round, circle, compasse, wheeling, revolution, circumuolution, vicissitude, interchangeable course of things; also, a turne, bout, or walke, as (we say) in Powles; also, the turne, course, ranke, place, or order, wherein a man is or stands; also, a deed, act, worke, part, good or bad Office, good or ill turne; also, a feat, pranke, tricke, sleight, shift, deuise; also, a spinning wheele; also, a Turne, or Turners wheele; or as* Tournoir; *also, a Turnepike, or Turning-stile; and the open turning box in the wall of a Nunnerie, wherby the sisters vnseeing, and vnseene, receiue in, and deliuer out, commodities; also, the Rooke at Chests; also, the breadth of fiue fingers in measure; also, a fashion of killing Deere, &c, by riding gently neere them, and hauing* en croupe *some Bowman, who may with aduantage, and on a sudden shoot at them.*

« *A Tour is a turn, round circle, compass, wheeling; also, a turne, bout, or walk; also, a deed, work, part, good or bad Office; also, the breadth of five fingers in measure; also, a fashion of killing Deere . . . by some bowman, who may with advantage and on a sudden shoot at them.* »

[Randle Cotgrave's *French-English Dictionary*, 1611.]

« tours »

Les mots

what is the word for bridge?
a solid structure made tenuous
the point at which one passes—
on foot « *passerelle* »
feminine—spanning shimmer

Les heures

it is not the venders
who open early
but the gardeners, planting
the morning « *le matin* » masculine—
in plural form, prayers
lauding the dawn—
& one woman, running
along the *rive* of unfamiliar

Les cartes

find her
au bord du Loire
seeds cottoning the air, two
boats, skeleton *&* cross bones
past *rue des quatre vents*
rue de la resistance
rib cage of wood
veering right where
trunk splits into wind

Les prépositions

forest above, below
in your mouth
flakes of language—
words are *mots* « leaves » *paroles*

Les questions

a steeple bell
rings cumulous
into the sky « *les nuages* »
what do they want to say?

if you ask one

who has left her village
she will respond
not *pourquoi* but *comment*
by boat, by horse, *à pied*

sole pressed to earth, no choice but—

Les fleurs

she wanders a garden of murmurs
happens upon two centuries
of alliance *provenance: Californie*

« *toujours vert* » always seen

in the country of origin
the trunk attains great heights
& a diameter of rings in circles

Les heures

armistice of the clock
la première guerre
mondiale—stopped

valuables on chariots
what they could not
take they broke

every woman was always
veuve—that is why *les Parisiennes*
always wear black

like everyone, I had
a grandmother, but not
a grandfather—that's also

very French—*mon amour*
le onze novembre
at the eleventh hour

the saint becomes his coat
hollyhock chapel
two rivers « *confluence* » under slate

Les questions

white stone
towers the quarries
white stone winds the roads

to a room that was

an « *oubliette* » of forgetting
source of every wailing
mon amour show me

again the place
where soldiers marked
zone of occupation

from *libre*—she once
played scales with
blindfolded hands

wished « *bon chance* »
to every root slender
lines under earth

binding *tous les morts*
to the living who return—
white stone in their mouths

Les cartes

& opposite the trees
à droite—little raised bed
of sad—*lá-bas*

river center, rain

drops into circles
inscribing *le ciel* *&*
the gull-flocked island

bird's eye, can you find
one wet face?

Les rues

streets named for
philosophers *&* doors
carved with flowers

revolution
in the square—

« *impasse des violettes* »
so many, one cannot pass
impossibility of color

Les verbes

not land cast into ocean but *jette*
current that wants to say motion
qu'est-ce que ça va dire?

heat rouges the poppies
doucement petals the air
in the language that was mine before

seul—her body
reverses over the bridge
limbs *proche*—gathering in

Les rues

we pass the *passage du coeur navré*
what is the value *mon amour?*
more than *désolée*
mind the steps
& the darkness
the false
dragon, iron rail
white stone *au coeur brisé*
fractured, broken « *blessé* »
wounded, not a blessing

Les fenêtres

closed hours, she
sees a woman
in glass *visage alto*—
small cello—cleft sides
wood held against
knees, genuflecting

Les questions

in the unfinished crypt
for burials & relics
we have no answers

only responses

underground, her breast
bleeding « *une apparition* »
tiny windows, pigeons

Les couleurs

the frogs chant
caché in the green wet
& yellow dots « *petits soleils* »
tended by bees

shocks of pink opening
rogue tremors
beneath the shadow of
an unknown tree

rendez-vous in the river
key that turns the belly
vertigo, secret passage of green

Les verbes

voler is to fly
or to steal
one's heart « *ailée* »

to have
an *alliance*
is a gold ring

worn on the hand
or to love
pour toujours

& the bird—
regarde
her open wingspan

Les phrases

ça rend me triste,
as in « that story makes
me »

j'ai besoin
as in « I need
you »

grâce à toi
as in « thanks
to »

il y a
as in « there are
quelque

choses » some things
like roots

« rending
their secret codes

BOOK III
OF KNOWINGS [GLOSSED & GLEANED]

[Honoré Bouvet instructs Christine to gather branches from his *Tree of Battles* in *The Book of Deeds of Arms and of Chivalry* BnF fol. 603, 49r.]

INSIDE THE TREE OF BATTLES: A DENDROCHRONOLOGY OF « DEEDS, ARMS & CHIVALRY »

A scribe does not simply write: [s]he copies & must have an exemplar from which to reproduce the text.[91]

... it is good for you to gather from the Tree of Battles in my garden some fruit that will be of use, so that vigor and strength may grow within you to continue work on the weighty book. ... You must cut some branches of this tree, taking only the best, and with this timber you shall set the foundation of this edifice.[92]

Every leaf in this forest
Will become a tongue to tell my story.[93]

The Golden Age: A time when « Men lived happily and in peace with the gods and each other. They did not kill and they had no locks on their doors, for theft had not yet been invented. »[94] We know of this time through philosophers and

---

[91] De Hamel, *Scribes and Illuminators*, 34.
[92] *The Book of Deeds of Arms and of Chivalry*, trans. S. Willard, 144.
[93] Philomela to Tereus, *Tales from Ovid*, trans. Hughes, 220.
[94] *D'Aulaires' Book of Greek Myths*, 14. Margolis explains the Golden Age for Christine's circle as representing a "poetic and historiographical theme, often nostalgic, signifying the pinnacle of a civilization, especially those of Greece . . . and Rome. . . . France,

poets who sang its existence. One tells of its demise after a god steals fire from his father to ease the suffering of mortals. We know the god as Prometheus and his punishment as imprisonment at the summit of a mountain, every day his liver devoured afresh by an eagle. As for the mortals: « The price for the stolen fire will be a gift of evil / to charm the hearts of all men as they hug their own doom. »[95]

The Age of Heroes: A prince is sent as an emissary to a foreign kingdom and received in the palace as guest. He returns home with the divinely beautiful wife of his host, a violation of the sacrosanct code of hospitality known as *xenia*, from the ancient Greek root ξένος meaning « guest, stranger, foreigner. »[96] We know the ensuing story as *The Iliad* and the burning of the prince's city as Troy.

First Century CE: Development of the Roman codex, replacing scrolls and wax tablets as the dominant technology for the making of books in the ancient world. Rooted in the Latin *caudex*, meaning « trunk of a tree » or « wooden tablet » or « code of laws », the codex allows for multiple points of
entry, rather than the sequential viewing required by unscrolling—the way we might perceive rings nested inside a cross-sectioned tree, each year a circled mark,

---

particularly Paris, through its poets and intelligentsia, promoted itself as « the second Athens. » " *An Introduction to Christine de Pizan*, 175.
[95] Hesiod, *Works and Days*, ll. 58–59, trans. N. Athanassakis, 66. D'aulare, 72–73.
[96] OED online.

each year visible all at once.[97] Constructed by the sewing together of sheets of pages, also known as *leaves*, we know its form each time we open a book in our hands.

14-37: A not particularly distinguished author who works for an emperor composes « a densely written, derivative, but very useful collection of historical anecdotes, many of dubious authenticity, titled *Factorum ac dictorum memorabilium libri IX* (*The Nine Books of Memorable Deeds and Sayings*), or *Facta et dicta.* »[98] Translated into French at the request of a king, the work will become known in the Middle Ages as « Valere-Maxime, *Faiz et ditz memorables.* »[99] We know the writer as Valerius Maximus and the style in which he wrote a « typical example of *Silver Latin*, a literary period often criticized for poor writers. »[100]

ca. 383-450: A Roman bureaucrat with no direct military experience compiles ideas from various sources to write a military treatise outlining essential policies, principles, and practices of warfare. His aim is to reform a Roman army fallen

---

[97] OED online.
[98] Margolis, *An Introduction to Christine de Pizan*, 197.
[99] Willard identifies the translators as Simon de Hesdin and Nicolas de Gonesse, *The Book of Deeds of Arms and of Chivalry*, 4. The king who engages the translation is Charles V.
[100] "Valerieus Maximus," *Wikipedia*, accessed 1 April 2017.

into corruption, but the guide he authors is widely used throughout the Middle Ages and continues to be highly regarded by military officers well into the nineteenth century. We know the author as Vegetius and the work as *De re militari*. One of its more famous maxims is: « He who desires peace should prepare for war. »

ca. 500: Salic law—known in Latin as *Lex Salica* and previously transmitted orally via a council of elders—is recorded at the behest of Clovis I, the first Frankish King. Copied by scribes over centuries, the code will serve as a basis of law throughout the Middle Ages that excludes women from inheritance of lands and thrones. We know the law from Act I, Scene II of Shakespeare's *Henry V*, in which the Archbishop of Canterbury spins letter, spirit, and practice to make a case for the English king's right to rule France: « Howbeit, they would hold up this Salique law / To bar your Highness claiming from the female . . . / For in the book of Numbers is it writ / When the man dies, let the inheritance / Descend unto the daughter. »

c. 1230: A French cleric named Guillaume de Lorris, of whom not much else is known, begins what will become one of the most popular texts of the Middle Ages, *The Romance of the Rose*. A chivalric tale of a young man who falls in love with a rose sheltered inside the fortified walls of a castle garden, the allegorical poem of four thousand lines will be taken up forty years later by a sharp-witted author who adds seventeen thousand lines to create a far darker version of « the art of love. »[101] We know the revisionist as Jean de Meun, and one illumination on a *Rose* manuscript leaf to look like this:

[« Amant penetrates the Rose » *Roman de la rose*, BUV, MS 387, f. 147v, Universitat de València, Biblioteca Històrica.][102]

---

[101] Known in Latin as *Ars amatoria*, Margolis notes that Ovid's classic treatise, *The Art of Love*, was "criticized by Christine in such works as the *God of Love's Epistle*."

[102] Also pictured in Desmond & Sheingorn, *Myth, Montage, & Visuality in Late Medieval Manuscript Culture*, 54.

1337: A generations-long rivalry begins over succession of the French throne and the largest kingdom in Western Europe. We know it as the Hundred Years' War, although the opposing dynasties won't declare a formal peace until twenty years after the last battle, marking its duration more accurately as a century and a half.

1364: A young prince from the cadet branch of the Capetian dynasty travels with his retinue to be anointed as the French monarch at the Cathedral of Reims. Three days before the coronation, his sister's husband mounts an attack in revolt over being denied royal territories through a maternal line. Known as *Charles the Bad* and backed by an army of some eight hundred knights and four thousand soldiers, including three hundredEnglish archers, the rebellious brother-in-law is soundly defeated by the military expertise of a Breton captain whom the new king—known as Charles *le Sage*—will make his chief military leader.[103] Twenty-three years later, suffering from fever, the insurgent will be wrapped in brandy-soaked sheets and accidently set afire in his own bed.[104]

1364-1380: Charles V reigns as King of France through his paternal lineage in the House of Valois. In addition to establishing a naval force, the Wise King will build

---

[103] The Battle of Cocherel is recounted by Christine in *Deeds and Good Practices of the Wise King Charles V* II.v, trans. G.McLeod in *The Writings of Christine de Pizan*, 239. C.C. Willard details the incident on page 247n.8.
[104] Tuchman, *A Distant Mirror*, 463.

a vast library of some twelve hundred volumes, the basis of today's *Bibliothèque nationale de France*. This grand bibliographic project includes the first translations into French of classical Latin works, such as Aristotle's *Ethics* and St. Augustine's *City of God*. Intended to demonstrate his royal prestige and political power, Charles's unprecedented campaign exemplifies the medieval concept of *translatio studii*—the transfer of learning from classical times—along with a parallel belief known as *translatio imperii*—the taking over by empire through inheritance of Golden Age virtue.[105]

Long after the sage ruler's death, a foreign-born widowed mother who will become known as the first woman commissioned to write a biography of a king, will praise « How King Charles Loved Books, and the Excellent Translations He Commissioned ».[106] By then, she will have gained access, not only to Aristotle and St. Augustine, but to translations of *Facta et Dicta*, *De re militari*, and all the other Golden Age teachings in the Wise King's library.

1365: A baby girl is born in Venice to a family from the Pizzano region of Italy. Her father, a respected professor at the University of Bologna, is invited to the French

---

[105] See, Margolis, 196, and Colman, "Reading the Evidence in Text and Image: How History Was Read in Late Medieval France" in *Imagining the Past in France*, 58.
[106] *Deeds and Good Practices of the Wise King Charles V* II.xii. trans. Willard in *Writings of Christine de Pizan*, 240.

court of the Wise King to serve as royal astrologer and physician. Known in his adopted country as Thomas de Pizan,[107] the father will move his young family to Paris, and at fifteen, his only daughter will marry a court notary with whom she will have three children. We know the girl as Christine de Pizan, and of this marriage she will write: « Our love and our two hearts were completely in accord . . . our two wills were one, whether it was a question of joy or of sorrow. »[108]

1380: Never in robust health, Charles V dies at age forty-four, leaving his eleven-year-old son, Charles VI—known as the Dauphin—to inherit the French throne. Because of the new monarch's youth, four ducal uncles oversee the kingdom, squandering royal funds and jockeying for power. Of this time, Christine will write: « As is usual when powerful men have died, great upheavals and changes come about in the condition of their courts and lands, caused by the clash of many opposing wills; and it can hardly be otherwise unless great wisdom prevents it . . . »[109]

---

[107] An inscription on the flyleaf of manuscript BnF fr. 606 parallels Christine's lineage with that of the House of Valois: « *L'epistre de Othea* was dedicated to Monsieur d'Orléans, son of King Charles V *&* written in French verse by Xpine, daughter of Master Thomas de Pizan, also called Thomas de Bologne. » Thanks to Sarah Wilma Watson for assistance in translation. Watson dates the inscription as likely seventeenth or eighteenth century. *The Othea* was composed by Christine around 1400.
[108] *The Path of Long Study*, trans. Brownlee, *Selected Writings of Christine de Pizan*, 62.
[109] *Christine's Vision*, trans. Blumenfeld-Kosinski, from modern French edition by C. Reno and L. Dulac, in *Selected Writings*, 186–87.

Charles VI, who will finally assert his rule as king at the age of twenty-one, will be known alternately as le *Bien-Aimé* (the Beloved) and *le Fou* (the Mad).

1387: Honoré Bouvet—known, alternatively, as Honorat Bovet or Bonet and a respected older contemporary of Christine's—composes a military-historical treatise called *L'Arbre des Batailles* (*Tree of Battles*) and dedicates it to the young King Charles VI. Basing his ideas of Just War on a long line of theological thinkers dating from Saint Augustine, Bouvet relies most immediately on the work of a Bolognese jurist known to have married into

the family of a renowned legal scholar at the university where Christine's father had taught before entering the Valois court.[110]

Of the famed legist, known as Giovanni Andrea, Christine will write: « He had a fair and good daughter, named Novella, who was educated in the law to such an advanced degree that when he was occupied . . . he would send Novella . . . in his place to lecture to the students from his chair. And to prevent her beauty from distracting the concentration of her audience, she had a little curtain drawn in

---

[110] Margolis identifies "the theologically based treatise on just war and peace" as John of Legnano's *Tractatus de bello* (*Treatise on War, Retaliation, and Combat*), 181-182. See, too, C.C. Willard, *Deeds of Arms and of Chivalry*, 4.

front of her. . . . He loved her so much that, to commemorate her name, he wrote a book of remarkable lectures on the law which he entitled *Novella super Decretalium*, after his daughter's name. »[111]

1389: Christine's father dies « at exactly the hour he had predicted » leaving little material wealth and « nothing to blame unless one counts the excessive generosity of refusing none of his possessions to the poor, although he had a wife and children. »[112] Fifteen years later, in a chapter titled « Here It Is Told How She Gathered Nothing but Scraps from Her Father's Treasure », Christine will write of another inheritance denied: her father's rich store of knowledge: « [B]ecause I was born a girl, it was not at all ordained that I should benefit in any way from my father's wealth. . . . If justice reigned, the female would lose nothing in this regard, nor would the son.[113]

1390: Christine's husband dies, leaving her with three children, her widowed mother, and a niece to support. Marking this devastating turn in a future codex, Christine will inscribe a reproach: « Ah, Fortune, what a treasure you took from me! My possibilities were greatly diminished when you did not let me keep those

---

[111] *City of Ladies*, trans. E.J. Rivers, 154.
[112] *Christine's Vision*, trans. Blumenfeld-Kosinski, *Selected*, 187.
[113] *Fortune's Transformation*, trans. Brownlee, *Selected*, 94.

two [father and husband] until I had advanced in learning. You harmed the very character of my soul! »[114]

1394-1405: Educating herself with books from the Wise King's library, Christine begins writing lyric poetry for noble patrons, including Isabeau of Bavaria, queen consort to Charles VI, whose capacity to rule will be devastated by illness known in the court as « absences. » As Christine's reputation grows, she composes increasingly bold works, engaging in a public debate that challenges one of the most popular texts of the Middle Ages as both misogynistic and without literary merit. We know the debate as the *Querellle des femmes*, and an illumination from one of the incendiary leaves to look like this:

---

[114] *Christine's Vision*, trans. C. C. Willard, *Writings*, 16.

[« Amant plucking the Rose » *Roman de la rose*, BUV, MS 387, f. 147v, 3. Universitat de València, Biblioteca Històrica.][115]

Of recovering for herself the rightful treasure of her father's wisdom, Christine will write: « Once a man criticized my desire for knowledge by saying that it was not fitting for a woman to possess learning because there was so little of it; I replied that it was even less fitting for a man to possess ignorance because there was so much of it. »[116]

---

[115] Also pictured in Desmond & Sheingorn, *Myth, Montage, & Visuality in Late Medieval Manuscript Culture*, 55.

[116] *Christine's Vision*, trans. Blumenfeld-Kosinski, 193.

1410: An Italian-born woman living in Paris—known in the fifteenth century as *the second Athens*—aligns herself with the Golden Age goddess Athena, a deity the Romans knew as Minerva, to forge works « durable as iron: neither fire nor anything else can destroy. »[117] As does her divine counterpart, the mortal female—whom we know as Christine—will engage in military matters, wielding her « tools and hammer on the anvil » to fashion not sword and shield but a book comprised of leaves:

« A book is not made up of single pages, but of pairs of leaves or bifolia. Several pairs of leaves are assembled one inside another, folded vertically down the middle and they can be stitched through the middle of the central fold to make a book in its simplest form. . . . Each clutch of folded bifolia is called a gathering or quire or signature. All standard medieval manuscripts are made up of gatherings. This is absolutely crucial. It is probably the single most important observation that can be made about the making of medieval books. »[118]

This particular book of Christine's—a treatise advancing theories, practices, and laws of just war—gathers together not only quires of leaves but the unmistakable signatures of Vegetius, Valerius Maximus, and Honorat Bouvet. In fact, the elder

---

[117] Ibid. Some of the language here is also drawn from Margolis, 95.
[118] De Hamel, *Scribes and Illuminators*, 18–19.

Bouvet appears as a character in Christine's book, urging her to gather freely from his *Tree of Battles*, despite her worry that her use will be viewed as theft:

« Dear friend, in this matter I reply that the more a work is seen and approved by people, the more authentic it becomes. Therefore, if anyone should murmur, according to the ways of detractors, saying that you took material from others, I answer them by saying that it is common usage among my disciples to exchange and share the flowers they take from my garden. . . . And even though they help themselves, they are not the first to do so. Did not Master Jean de Meun make use of the works of Lorris, and likewise of other writings in his *Romance of the Rose*? It is therefore not a rebuke, but a lawful and praiseworthy matter for therein is the indication of having seen and read many books. But it is wrong to take material without acknowledgement; therein is the fault. So do boldly what you have to do and do not doubt that your work is good. I assure you that it shall be commended and praised by many a wise man. »[119]

Known in Middle French as *Le Livre des Fais d'armes et de chevallerie* and in modern English as *The Book of Deeds of Arms and of Chivalry*, Christine's book will indeed

---

[119] *The Book of Deeds of Arms and of Chivalry*, trans. S. Willard, 144.

become widely regarded as an exemplar of military ethics and skillful practice.[120] And while the iron-forged signature of its author will often be erased, one codex—now known as British Library Harley MS 4605—will depict Golden Age deity and medieval mortal, in an indelible lineage, side by side on folio three:

[« Christine in her study, writing, and standing outside to the right, the goddess Minerva, armored, crowned, and carrying a sword and shield. » *Le livre des faits*

---

[120] *The Book of Feats of Arms and Chivalry* is another accepted translation of the title. As Margolis points out (247n.68), *Deeds* is the rendering in the complete translation by Sumner Willard, which also serves as the generative text for the sequence of lyrical erasures that follow this essay.

d'armes et de chevalerie, scribed in French by Delafita in London, 1434. BL Harley MS 4605, f. 3r.]^[121]

1412: Another girl is born in a small village in northeastern France. As a child, she watches her village burn, set afire by raiding soldiers. We know the village as Domrémy and the girl as Joan of Arc, sometimes called the Maid of Orléans, after the village she will liberate from a months-long siege by occupying forces. In France, she is often called *la Pucelle*. *Une pucelle* can be any girl, maid, or virgin, while *putain* always means *whore*, employed also as an expletive, abbreviated sometimes to *pute*. Before she is burned for restoring the crown to a French king's head, *la Pucelle* will give testimony of a forest in Domrémy, known as the Polled Wood:

« [Y]ou can see it from my father's door, it is not half a league away. I never heard that the fairies met there. But it had been prophesied that a maid would come from near that wood to do wonderful things. But I said I had no faith in that. »[122]

---

[121] Online at the British Library Catalogue of Illuminated Manuscripts. Enlarged, the image also serves as the cover of Margolis' *An Introduction to Christine de Pizan*, where one might easily trace the diagonal line of Minerva's green leaves as they reconfigure to become the tiled floor upon which Christine composes her book.

[122] Joan of Arc, *In Her Own Words*, trans. Trask, 5.

The Golden Age: Two gods disguised as mortals knock on the weathered door of a humble cottage.[123] They are welcomed by an elderly couple who, despite their poverty, treat the strangers with generous hospitality, according to the ancient code of guest-friendship known as a *xenia*. In return for their
reverence, the devoted pair are spared the punishing flood suffered by their unobservant neighbors whose doors had remained bolted against the disguised travelers, sometimes known as Zeus and Hermes, sometimes as Jupiter and Mercury.

As the story is known, the two surviving elders, known as Baucis and Philemon, live out their remaining years guarding the temple of the god who knocked as a stranger, and when the hour arrives for their passing, their long-held prayer is granted: to remain united, even as their human forms depart the earth.

> Baucis saw Philemon come into leaf,
> and Philemon saw Baucis put forth leaves.
> Then, as their faces both were covered over
> by the growing treetop, while it was allowed them,
> they spoke and answered one another's speech:
> « Farewell, cherished one » they both cried out together,
> just as their lips were sealed in leafiness.

---

[123] Ovid, *Metamorphoses*, Book VIII.863–1000, trans. Martin.

1965: A girl is born in the shadow of mountains named after an angel known as Gabriel. One day as a child, she rides a public school bus to visit the grounds of great wealth. Situated in splendid gardens over acres of land, a grand library stores a tremendous cache of rare books, hundreds of codices purchased at great cost. Among them is Christine's *Book of Arms and Chivalry*, signed by the mother of a king.[124]

It will be years before the girl knows of this treasure made of paper leaves and ink, but one day she will relay the story of the devout Golden Age couple who treated beggars like kings. One day, she will think back on that journey away from her own small home by the mountains and wonder how a future codex might transfer *learning* into *peace* rather than *conquest*.

One day she will find herself in the forest of a foreign land, where a stranger who has gone before will teach her how to read at once the marked rings and the silent wood nestled in between: *heartwood, pith, cambium layer*.[125] And in the language of her host, she will deploy an inheritance of questions, starting with: *What might it*

---

[124] The Huntington Library is home to a printed copy of the volume signed by Margaret Beaufort, mother of King Henry VII. Thanks to Sarah Wilma Watson for information regarding provenance and current location.

[125] "Anatomy of a Tree" *Arbor Day Foundation*.

mean for a young girl to look out the windows of borrowed transport and see castles? To gaze up at a stand of golden-leafed aspens and imagine young soldiers?

~

[Lower cross section of Christine's *Livre des faiz d'armes et de chevalerie*, BnF fr. 1183. View 462 – Folio tranche inférieure. *People also ask: What does tranche mean in English?* « In French, *tranche* means "slice." Cutting deeper into the word's etymology, we find the Old French word *trancer*, meaning "to cut." *Tranche* emerged in the English language in the late nineteenth century to describe financial appropriations. . . . Another use of the French word *tranche* is the French phrase *une trance de vie*, meaning "a cross section of life." » Quoted from Merriam-Webster Dictionary, est 1828; accessed online via Google Chrome, 2023.]

« leavings »

My mistress summons   the immortal of her courage

~~   **B**efore the book began
paired leaves   folded
a gathering   a quire   a signature

Leaves of flesh   pared from
skin   pelt stretched taut
circulus   *lunellum*

~~   Before the book began
an immortal   sprang whole
from the head of her father

Born bearing weapons
she took shape as
a woman   an owl

High   in the ink-black cypress
she watched   the son
of a king   steal treasure

Swan-throated wife   torn
from her children   as a wolf
caught   chews its flank

On her fury-forged anvil
wing   melded   to shield
timber   blackened to battle

Before the book began   ~~
poets sang the story

Of ships   carrying armaments
arrow   catapult   sling
a country   of men &

Before the book began   ~~
they stormed   the walled city
burned ramparts   every   tree

Before the book began   ~~

A woman born on water
carved a knife   from a feather

Recto   verso   she inscribed
leaves of skin
with war

~~

[Floating ink endpaper. « Title: *Livres des faiz d'armes et de chevalerie*. Subject: Art militaire. Publication date: 1401-1500. » BnF, fr. 1183, View 2 - Folio contreplat sup.]

i. Here begins   so bold   the book
                                                                Nothing
              risked   to set forth

my unworthiness   exalted ~   dared
                                           blameworthy   fool-
hardy   I   inspired
                                    presumption   genuine desire
of men engaging in   arms   ~ I
                                            undertake to speak
                  as   builder
                                 bold   .   to construct a castle
or fortress
                       I have gathered   from
              books   this volume ~
                             polished words
expert language
                     the plainest possible ~~
                                        Unusual women
                                                              weaving
spinning   I   invoke   speaking
                                             Wisdom ~
                     the poet praises her
                                                              trap-
pings   iron *&* steel
                          Let the works be good ~~
                                                        Forging
              helmets shields   protective covering
I undertake
                              to speak
                                        from   the country beyond
where you were born

169

ii. How wars & battles   just   &   proper

        Valiant warrior
                        make use of   writings   doc-
trine   discipline of arms   composed & bound
                                                        what-
ever   may   endure   written lasts
         forever   ~
                it is a matter of no small consequence   ~
                                                   to learn whether
                               great
                      wrongs   extortions   rapine
killings   forced   & arson ~
          manifest   just cause ~
             proof of   Holy Writ
                                    ordered
      an ambush
                             of God
   Lord & Governor of Hosts & battles
                         execution of justice ~
               Divine law   drawn   by
people
    outside   right
              evil will
                      touch

iv. Concerning   causes

                consider   lawful
                      grounds   commonly held
                                             ~
                          justice   evildoers
who   injure & oppress
                              under   jurisdiction of
     ~ avenge
                     damage   conquer   ~~
A king
      empowered to   wars & battles ~
                                   patrimony
       on behalf of
                 a quarrel   is
           adversary   intractable ~
                               justly   aid   any
ally & friend ~
            widows orphans   trampled   by
power ~~
       Counteract   recover
               obligation
                       proper duty ~~
                                        Acquisition
       without title
                   chivalric
                         wreaked
                                 ground ~~
Vengeance   reserved for   ~~
                        divine
                  sovereign
                          realm

[*Livre des faiz d'armes et de chevalerie*, BnF, fr. 1183, fol. NP]

ix. How   antiquity instructed   children

                 the practice of arms   continued
                         ~ sons
     fourteen onward
                            taught to
wear armor   take care   in combat ~~
                        Vegetius speaks   the fourth
             chapter   imbue
     what is shown   by nature
                            wrestle   jump &
play
       tricks of agility   striking   sidestep
blows   leap   ditches   throw darts
     protect with   shield ~   They
                 should be shown   the left foot
forward   body
      steadied   thrust of   weapon
hand-to-hand   swords   forward
       falling   confusion ~
                      victors
        put as companions
               to defend   each other   as if
    castles ~~

x. More of the same

      how   a sling
           defends a mountain   ~
                  some   *would not give food to their children*
            until they   struck   meat with a slingshot blow ~
      how to
      hold the bow
arrow near   ear   heart *&* eye   on the mark
                young
                          archers ~
this art must be practiced
                          throw stones   bear shields
                    throw lances ~
                                    take note
                the bodies of youths
          agile
                alert   spirits flexible
      chest   shoulders   arms
          hands   bellies   backs   thighs
                                                  the
body   immaterial   ~~
        Along with this   swim rivers   the sea ~~
                          Wounded   alone
                                            with
night ~   the ancients ~~
                  Say
                          All things   *diffcult*
become easy ~

[A castle under siege in the *Livres de Faits d'armes et de chevalerie*, authored by Christine and illuminated by the Maître de la Cité des Dames with secondary decoration attributed to « la vigne d'or », or, the Golden Vine, 1410–11. BnF, fr. 603, fol. 27v.]

xvii. The crossing of rivers & streams

                   filled with   deep ~   a line of men
between~
             the water's force   empty barrels
                                      drawbridge   skill   of
artisans ~
       stakes   in water   ropes
              planks~
                   boats
                       reeds
                           firmly anchored ~   By such means
the king   devised solutions
                           by the River
                                     impossible ~
       excavating the earth   di-
   vided   streams   crossed
      over
       ~~
                     Histories
swimming   broad rivers   wood hollowed
     branches   a bridge
                             of arrows ~~
                                           Things
                     imagined ~
                                  wide   regions
     no boats   on the banks ~
if it happens   possible   moon-
           light
                 escape through mountains   ~
paths   barred by woods
                 cut a way   by hand

xviii. When   battle is imminent

speak of certain
books of arms
authors who have written   ~
attack
trampled   foot ~
hasten
full scale
~ foolish   wise   valiant
~   malcontent
courtly   military ~
marvelous
ambushed
mountains
a thousand
elephants   ~
cross rivers
swamps   narrow passages
arrange
formation ~
avoid
encampments   ~
~~   History tells us
~~   Desperate
men
die fighting
the cruel ~
a small number   have often
a great multitude   ~~
Note
your advantage or   regret   & do nothing

xxi. The   day before   battle
                                                war leads
              to   formation   essential
                                              combat
                          obliged   assemble   the face
the wise commander must not fail
                          fortunes of all land   state
                    life infinite ~~
                          Summon commanders
brothers   companions
                    to protect & hold
                                sustain by   sword   just quarrel
recompense   life & limb
                          promised   oaths   deserting death
          stout hearts
                    profit
                          merit ~~
     Such words   the wise   say to   men
                                         in accord with
                                                conquerors
books of chivalry   recommend
                                        honor
                    His enemy
          silver vessels
                    only   wooden bowls
                                        eat honorably
          shame & reproach   golden dishes~
                                         generosity &
kindness   embolden
                          humble soldiers
                                   written valiant ~~
          Pleasing words are useful for this purpose

[A manuscript leaf ornamented with foliage blooms. « Image: Presentation. Author: Flavius Vegetius Renatus, trans. Jean de Meun. Title: *Les establissemenz de chevalerie* (a French translation of *De re militari*). Date: 1st half of the fifteenth century. Script: Gothic cursive. Form: Parchment codex. Provenance: John Shirley author, translator, and scribe (b. c. 1366, d. 1456) : his monogram and motto . . . » British Library MS Royal 20 B XV, f. 2]

[Vegetius III xxii]

                                              :   sweet   inexperienced
                                                    ~
                          You will know   warriors   afraid of fighting ~~

[trans. Milner]

xxii. Advantage   the field according to

                                                                                 words *&* the movements
                    of   ~   fear
                                      loyal captains
                                                                       position
                    by   flight
                                obedient
      a single voice
                                the ancients
made use of certain signs
                                               trumpets
        horns   bugles   otherwise
                                            heat of battle
                  sounds   need ~~
Advantage   the terrain ~   three points
                    :   first   the high place   second
at the hour of combat ~~
                  Sun in the eyes dazzles
                                & the arrow carried by wind
                      ruses
               time

xxiv. The order & arrangement of battles

                        the ancients   say
                                    a circle ~
                                                        Where
            expected ~
                       serrated
                              vulnerable ~
horseshoe ~
         alter
                 the line up ~
                             distance & space
                                               fall apart ~
                              light
broken   scattered ~~
                        Certain
                              squares &   triangles
                   reformed ~
                            defeat
                       hope   the opposite of
          great slaughter ~~
                      on either side ~~
                                        Courage   troubled
                           trumpet call ~
     fleeing   fighting   ~~
                                     Then   heavy rain
          cords   loosened
       ropes
               castles filled with water ~
In this way
          the territory
                     gained victory

xxv. Ways of drawing   an army

The first   marshaling   the field
                                              ~ a difficult terrain   easily
                          broken ~~
The second   ~
                                        begin   with
                                outflanking ~
              the letter X
                          a great number
                                         oppose   with great
                    force
~~ Third
              your left wing ~
                                    joins
         the right   of your enemy
                                         ~ neither swords or missiles
              ~ take care   not
                                    to break
                    ~~
The fourth :   when you have ordered
                    five hundred
                                         unprepared ~
      & divided
                                    the middle   from its wings ~~
The fifth ~
                    put   to flight
                          archers ~~
                                    your army ~
                    cannot be rescued
                                    like   part of the letter L   far
              removed

[« Miniature of a battle between fully armed men on foot, with on the right, a man pouring blood out of a jug onto a stand of trees; probably refers to the bloodsoaked 'Tree of Battles' of Honoré Bovet's L'Arbe des batailles » *Le livres des faits d'armes et de chevalerie*. England, 1434. BL Harley 4605, f. 41.]

xxvi. More of the same

The seventh way   is this   :
                            take possession
                                            of sea   mountains ~
                                                                           put
forward the bravest   ~~   However few

xxvii. When fortune is favorable

                                                                     the enemies
                                                                                               killed ~
              like animals   ~
                          courage   broken   fear
                                                                       ~   pursue
to the end   ~
                          great loss   not   known
                                                                        to resist

xxviii. When   fortunes   turn against

       boldness   changed to fright ~

                                                            a trap

laid ~

                   in

          courage   ~

                             sometimes

       chance

               descends on

                           ~   vanquished

                  conquerors

xxix. A brief recapitulation

~~ Bravery   more
                than force   ~~
      little hope   half-vanquished
                                            ~~   Chance gives victory
         ~~
        impossible to foresee

Part IV.   **Of**   **the most noble colors**

                                 exalted &   richest

               corresponding   to

nature ~

           gold   bright & shining

                 sovereign comfort

    unto death   ~

               nothing is more noble than light

                             ~

                 the just   shines like   the sun ~

      ~~

BOOK IV
OF LANGUAGES [SILENT & VOICED]

[« Illuminated by leaves, Christine writes »
The Book of Fortune's Mutation, BnF, fr. 603, fol. 81v.]

TRANSLATING LIGHT

> *Christine de Pizan comes from elsewhere: first of all, from another language.*[126]

> *Linguistic hospitality, therefore, is the act of inhabiting the word of the Other paralleled by the act of receiving the word of the Other into one's own home, one's own dwelling.*[127]

1]   Over six hundred years ago, a young foreign-born widow wrote about struggling to feed her kids, wearing a patched-up coat to do battle with creditors, putting off sexual advances without disgruntling anyone in power. She wrote not in the language of her birth, but in the language of the country she made home.

2]   For her early lyric poetry, Christine took as her model the poetic *formes fixes* outlined by Eustache Deschamps in his *Art de dictier* (*The Art of Writing Poetry*), a leading authority of the era, along with Guillaume de Machaut, who pioneered the French poetic vernacular.[128] At the same time, Christine re-imagined

---

[126] Cerquiglini, "The Stranger," in *The Selected Writings of Christine de Pizan*, 265, trans. Blumenfeld-Kosinski.
[127] Ricoeur, *On Translation*, xvi, trans. Kearney.
[128] Margolis, *An Introduction to Christine de Pizan*, 185.

conventional courtly themes—previously engaged with idealized notions of chivalric love—to convey the deep bonds of a happy marriage and the piercing loss of widowhood.

3]   In a letter dated February 10, 1404, Christine wrote to Deschamps, twenty years her senior: "Your great reputation has encouraged me, dear master and friend, to send you this. . . . if you would like to see examples of my little understanding in my works, you can order them, without special inquiries for I'm looking for your comments." Deschamps responded graciously with kind encouragement, likening Christine to one of the nine muses and thanking her "a hundred times" for her letter, "received with great joy."

Their exchange, translated into English by Renate Blumenfeld-Kosinski,[129] reminds me of Emily Dickinson's letter to Thomas Wentworth Higginson, written over four hundred years later in another language, another country: "Are you too deeply occupied to say if my verse is alive? The mind is so near itself it cannot see distinctly, and I have none to ask."

---

[129] *Selected Writings*, 109–13.

Both women, extraordinary in their work, felt alone in their undertaking. And they were. Both wrote themselves into a literary world inhabited by men, and in doing so, expanded that world for others through the newness and possibility of their language.

4]   One day, fortune brought me into the gracious presence of a community who brought the possibility of Christine into language I knew how to read. One translator, a preeminent scholar of medieval French and Italian literature, answered my most basic of questions as if they were the most critical he had ever heard.

Q. *Do you think Christine spoke Italian at home with her mother?*
A. *Well, hmmm. We can't know for certain, but yes, yes. I imagine she did.*

Q. *Do you think Christine ever wanted to marry again?*
A. *Well now, let me think about that some more.*

5]   Christine often referred to herself as *seulete*, a woman alone, small and of little consequence in comparison to the male *auctours* of her time. In a time and place unaccustomed—even hostile—to solitary women, Christine undertook to produce manuscripts for royals. That her books are read and studied centuries

after their making is its own small miracle. In part, it was achieved through Christine's own brilliance and fortitude. In part, it was the support of those in power who helped her—and the translators who continue to bring her writing into language anew.[130]

6] The first time I saw Christine's name, it was inside a book I happened upon while wandering a library I had permission to enter. On page 284:

CHRISTINE DE PIZAN (c.1365-c.1430)
"Those Things I Have Here Refuted"
See also **Vision** and **Transformation**.

As fortune would have it, one of the editors of that particular book has an office at the university where that particular library is located.[131]

---

[130] The first full-length translation into English of *Le Livre de la Mutacion de Fortune* was published as recently as March of 2017 by Geri Smith under the title: *The Book of the Mutability of Fortune*. Renate Blumenfeld-Kosinski and Earl Jeffrey Richards' *Othea's Letter to Hector* was published in 2017, thirty years after Jane Chance's translation of the *Epistre Othéa* into English.

[131] Natania Meeker, Associate Professor of French and Comparative Literature at the University of Southern California, is one of three editors of *Women Imagine Change*.

7]   *Translatio studii* is Latin for the **transfer of learning**. The term might also be understood as **knowledge transfer**.[132]

8]   In learning how to write poetry, Christine practiced the *formes fixes* of the *ballade* and the *rondeau*. Both make appearances in « widow rounds », with the Middle French versions found in the first volume of *Oeuvres poétiques de Christine de Pisan*, edited by Maurice Roy and published in 1891. Christine's originals date to 1396, and are included in *The Queen's Manuscript* of 1414, along with the *Epistre Othéa* and the *Proverbes Moraux*, which date to 1400 and 1405, respectively.

When I first searched for the Roy volumes, they were missing from the library shelves. But they found me soon enough, as did the codex of a queen.[133]

9]   *Poetry comes to know that things are. But this is not knowledge in the strictest sense; it is, rather, acknowledgment—and that constitutes a sort of unknowing.*[134]

---

[132] See Colman, "Reading the Evidence in Text and Image," in *Imagining the Past in France*, 55.

[133] *Oeuvres poétiques de Christine de Pisan* are available online through Gallica, the digital library of the Bibliothèque nationale de France. *The Queen's Manuscript* is hosted online by the British Library as BL MS 4331, with detailed information available through the collaborative digital project, *The Making of the Queen's Manuscript*.

[134] Hejinian, *The Language of Inquiry*, 2.

10]   When I first saw Christine's name, French was not a language I knew well. Nor do I still. Poetry was the language that brought us together. Marina made translation possible. She refused silence to what is unknown.[135] Whether she translated me or I translated her, I cannot say.

11]   *The work of translation might thus be said to carry a double duty: to expropriate oneself as one appropriates the other. We are called to make our language put on the stranger's clothes at the same time as we invite the stranger to step into the fabric of our own speech.*[136]

See also **Vision** and **Transformation**. [number 6, above]

12]   An English translation of *Proverbes Moraux* was printed by William Caxton in 1478, a copy of which is currently housed at the Henry E. Huntington Library, across town from where I live in Los Angeles. To gain permission to enter the library requires knowledge of many sorts, including fluency in the language of bureaucratic forms. To gain access to the Caxton volume online requires only kind guidance of one who knows how, which is its own kind of knowledge transfer.

---

[135] See Spivak, *The Politics of Translation*, 200.
[136] Kearney, "Ricoeur's Philosophy of Translation," *On Translation*, xvi.

How *The Queen's Manuscript* came to be transported across the sea is a story for another day, but as fortune would have it, the translator for the Caxton volume was Anthony Woodville, the 2nd Earl of Rivers, who was executed by his own country's troubled leader, Richard, Duke of Gloucester (later, known as Richard III).

Christine's *Proverbes* number one hundred and one, and « moëttes » makes use of the first ten, with my translations appearing on the left-hand side, and Marina's inventions on the right. Christine's section was translated with assistance from Randle Cotgrave's *Dictionairie of the French and English Tongues*, printed in 1611 by Adam Islop of London and made available online from "two scans assembled in the French National Library" by Greg Lindahl. Whether these scans were made with permission, I do not know.

13]   *The Epistle of Othea to Hector, or, The Boke of Knyghthode Translated from the French of Christine de Pisan With a Dedication to Sir John Fastolf, K.G.* can also be found in the Huntington collection, although it's far more accessible online through the collaborative endeavor of The Getty Research Institute and the HathiTrust Digital Library.[137] That translation was made by Stephen Scrope *from a manuscript*

---

[137] The Mission Statement for HathiTrust states: "In addition to its primary focus on the HathiTrust Digital Library, HathiTrust and its partner institutions collaborate on some major initiatives to improve access to and promote preservation of scholarly materials both digital and print, in a variety of formats."

in the library of the Marquis of Bath and published in 1904 by J.B. Nichols and Sons, London. More recent translations include those by Earl Jeffrey Richards, Renate Blumenfeld-Kosinski, and Jane Chance, all of which I drew upon to compose « interscriptions ».

Translation, or "translacion" as she calls it, is not a neutral subject for Christine. She will never write in Italian, but her native language exists within her like a source or a potential resource.[138]

English—my language of birth—was the language of composition, what translation theorists call the **target** language, but the language from which I translated wasn't the Middle French of Christine. The **source** language was illumination. Which might be to say: *The light comes in the name of the voice (in nomine vocis venit claritas).*[139]

        See also **Vision** and **Transformation**. [number 6, above]

Q. But how does one gain access to light?
A. One country opens its library to the world.[140]

---

[138] Cerquiglini, 265.
[139] Carson, "Variations on the Right to Remain Silent," in *Float*.
[140] In October 2023, the British Library suffered a devastating cyberattack, disrupting access to online collections, including the ones that made this work possible. As of August, 2024, the BL reports that "the outage is still affecting our website, online

14]   The *ballade* and *rondeau* of Christine's poetic apprenticeship emerged out of dance and song traditions; as portrayed in *The Queen's Manuscript* of 1414, their lyrical music depended not on punctuation cues, but on an understood knowledge of the forms.¹⁴¹ The question then became: How might I convey this music to the unfamiliar while carrying over a sense of the manuscript original? Maybe more urgently: How might the voice of the woman who composed these poems resonate six hundred years after the keen grief that compelled their making?

*To know that things are is not to know what they are, and to know that without what is to know otherness (i.e., the unknown and perhaps unknowable).*¹⁴²

Translation allowed me to enter the music of that voice more deeply, in what Earl Jeffrey Richards recalls as *the here and now*. What remains constant: To hear a voice that sings across time and space is to understand our own experiences have always been shared by others. Maybe this is one way translation expands the possibility for knowing, the capacity for compassion.

---

systems, and services, as well as some onsite services, however our buildings are open as usual." https://www.bl.uk/cyber-incident/
¹⁴¹ Depicted as the frontispiece of « widow rounds ».
¹⁴² Hejinian, 2.

Puis me prist aux livres des pouetes, et comme de plus en plus, alast croiscent le bien de ma congnoiscence. [Then I occupied myself with the books of the poets, and more and more the measure of my knowledge increased.][143]

Q. And the woman who called herself *seulete*?
A. *Yes, now that you ask. Yes, I think she married poetry.*

Illuminated by the flame, we are never alone.

* * *

---

[143] Richards, *Christine de Pizan and Medieval French Lyric*, 215–16.

[*Proverbes mouraulx*, BnF, fr. 605, fol. 4r]

« moëttes »

1

Good merit and notable wisdom
Often return their profits.

So says my mistress, a lady
Whose hands held only ash.

2

Prudence attends the man who lives in reason,
There where she is happy is the house.

And blackness haunts the room
Where Fortune leaves the door ajar.

3

Men, temperate and cool-headed,
Cannot be but long measured.

Look not to collect those waters
Falling over shadowed ages.

4

Stout courage, constant and affirmed,
Is neither slight nor soon badly hurt.

Endurance stands where one has lost
Courage to run a blade along the wrist.

5

Where neither peace nor justice reign
Neither can last, so long as a grand ruler.

When he who reigned her heart crumbled
The sun descended forever.

6

Impossible to be a faithless creature
And pleasing to God, says Scripture.

Without Faith
None can find her treasure.

7

Favorable to the world and to God acceptable
Can no man be, if not charitable.

Charity accepts all Godly creatures
Whose conduct favors the world.

8

Hope guides the deeds of humans
But holds not her promises by the hand.

The body that searches the heavens
Tumbles down the stairs.

9

Glory lies not in great estates
But in Virtue's double memory.

The day glory & greatness lay together
Is the day Virtue is wed.

10

Cruel prince and robber of money—
I hold to folly those who trust his glove.

So says my mistress, a lady
Whose hands Fortune gloved in ash.

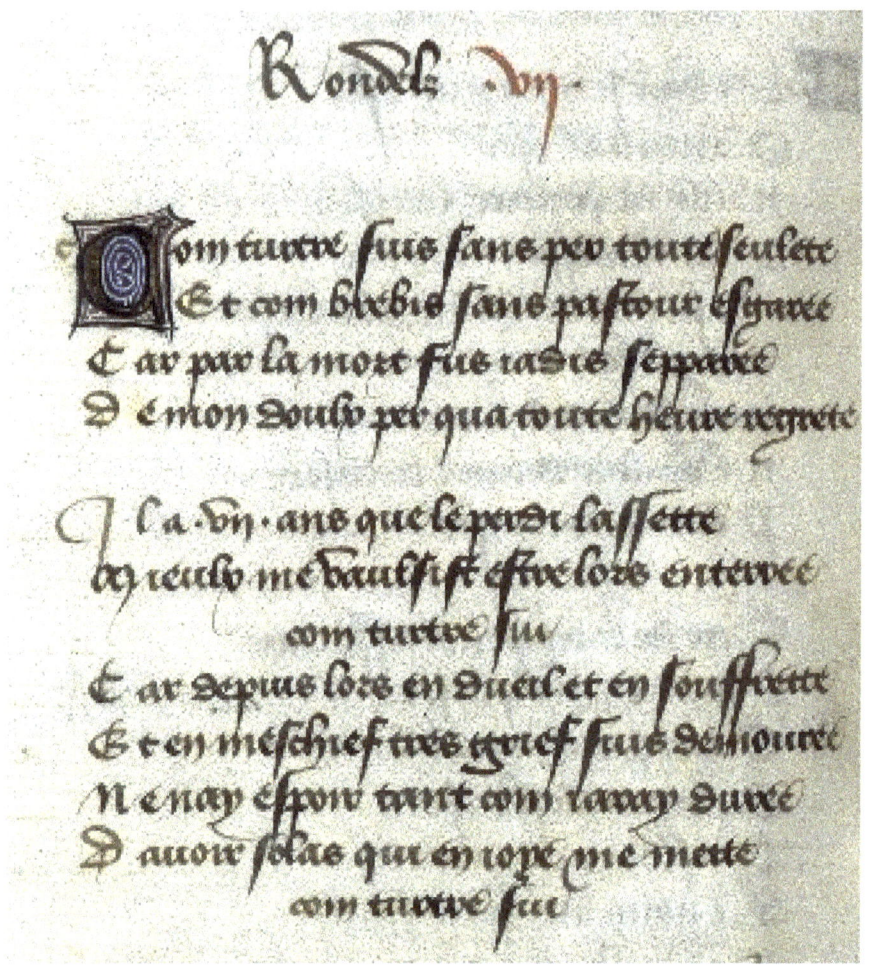

[The first *rondeau* as it appears in Harley MS 4431 [fol. 28v.], also known as *The Queen's Manuscript* and presented in 1414 by Christine de Pizan to Isabeau of Bavaria, queen consort of Charles VI. Christine is believed to have scribed some of the passages.]

« widow rounds »

i

Like a turtle dove   without her mate   am I
                                — entirely   alone
Lamb   without shepherd   wandering afield
Far from   death   who severed
My sweetest part   all hours   spent longing —

Seven years   wearied   by losing
Better to be   with you   buried
      Like a turtle dove   left solitary   am I

Disarrayed by mourning   left
Wanting   & in grief's meanness   I abide
Never hoping —   so long as I endure
      To have solace   or a place of joy —
As a turtle dove   without her mate   am   I

v

O enduring Death

                    you pulled from my crown

All my gold days

                    my most enduring substance

When you withdrew

                    he who was charged with

All my goodness

                    & my sustenance

So low am I placed

                    I swear to you —

I desire only to be

                    taken from my body

My wretched soul

                    bound to darkness

Since the one

                    who tethered me to

Life is buried —

1.12] Here is told how she lost the master of her ship

The Book of Fortune's Transformation

he who knew well how to interpret the Pole Star & how to trim the sails

to keep a straight course

darkened sky   cloud thick

crow's nest

disfigure my heart & face

corkscrew caught

whirlwind twist   violent into the sea

he who used to guide the ship   night & day through

all encumbrances & difficulties

I would have thrown myself   as Alcyone   lost Ceyx

held back   my heart ready

the very air trembled   with shouts   yells

bitter lamentations   deep sufferings

he   who was such a good pilot

such a loyal lover   there would never be

another   safe port

grief removed all fear   my voice pierced the heavens
consolation   devastated   hopeless of   earthly solace
our desolated ship   I could never again navigate

on that sea   on the wrong side   of happiness

**

I have since   been on land

Fortune took pity   but her help   I do not know
if it was more   of a danger

wearied by long crying   I fell asleep early —
she palpated   & took in her hands   each bodily part
then departed   our ship   following the waves of the sea
struck with great force   against a rock

I awakened   *&* felt myself   transformed

limbs stronger   myself bewildered

flesh   strengthened   my voice much lowered   *&* my

body   harder *&* faster

Hymen's ring   fallen from my finger   —   I found my heart   strong *&*

bold   amazed at this strange adventure

I saw the sail *&* mast   bad weather   smashed

the ropes *&* the tops   our ship broken   water streaming

I set to repair   with nails *&* pitch   *&* strong hammering   I

gathered moss   among the rocks   *&* put

into holes   until watertight   I rejoined the broken edges

thus I became a true man (this is no fable)

Fortune taught me this trade

until death   I continue my life

extricated from the rocks   my ship

& set off   toward the place   I started out —

XXIX

Il me semble qu'il a cent
Que mon ami de moy parti!

Il ara quinze jours par temps,
Il me semble qu'il a cent ans!

Ainsi m'a anuié le temps,
Car depuis lors qu'il departi
Il me semble qu'il a cent ans!

xxix

It seems to me a century

My love has from me parted

Fifteen days by time's measure

Each one seems a hundred years —

Such does my time grow late

Since the time

                my love departed

It seems to me one hundred lives

LIII

Cest anelet que j'ay ou doy
Mon doulz ami le m'a donné.

Souvent nous assemble toudoy
Cest anelet que j'ay ou doy.

Je l'aime bien, faire le doy;
Car pour ma joye est ordené
Cest anelet que j'ay ou doy.

liii

This ring around my finger

My sweetest love placed on me

Everlasting   it joins us together

This ring encircling my finger

I love it well — this ring

My joyfulness sealed forever

By this ring circled round my finger

My mistress recalls the presence of her beloved

Your hands not on the table resting
        but already on the page : inexplicable
yearning adorns us at once. However
        else touch is apprehended, one can
listen for the scent of *champignons*, just
        inside a tall oak door. A font of
snow quiets mountains, minerals tincture
        saints leafed in gold. They garden shadows
lit by lemons. The sun does not always
        announce her arrival, the painter does
not always leave a signature. Your hand
        wrote me from a distant corner
how one can hear sixty voices enter a multitude
        of cathedral arches. We do
sound every bell over ancient green
        assemblages. Pray how we were never
parted, my hand folded always into yours.

[Joan of Arc drawn in the margin of the protocol of the parliament of Paris, May 10, 1429, by Clement of Fauquembergue. French National Archives.]

« interscriptions »

[« Othea gives a letter to Hector; Temperance adjusts her clock » *Épître d'Othéa* BnF, fr. 848 fol. 2r.]

The imagined goddess gives her letter to the young warrior

By my letter   I wish to counsel
you   so that your good heart
addresses itself

so that   you may acquire

the horse which   takes flight
in the air

loved by   all the valiant

As goddess I know
things to come   it remains
to me   to remind you

always you will be

the most   of all expert
truly believe in me

Put well into your memory
the deeds   I wish to pass
souvenirs in the spirit

of prophecy   Now listen

for I shall say nothing
that will not come to pass

If it does not happen   you will remember it —

[*Épître d'Othéa*, BnF fr. 606, fol. 23v.]

Coronis   pierced by the flèche of Apollo

her   chest
treasure   opened

bodkin point   to shaft

keep with all watchfulness —

an arrow
rewards the telling

afterward   he would repent of it
the hand & bow   his

face   aflame
over the pyre   her crimson flares

whenever night   eclipses day

& where the tongue is quick
a dove becomes its opposite

ô ire-blackened raven   whose

breath windmills truth   fly silent
into sinew   belly stretched

guardian of the unborn   who
sutures   all wounds

[*Épître d'Othéa*, BnF, fr. 606, fol. 13v.]

Ceres sowing   Isis grafting trees

they float   above the earth
seeding the lost   harvest
      tilling without plough

keepers of our green   who

join stock   to shoot
rending flower   from knowledge
      tree of fruit —

offer freely   your daughters
before they are torn   ungleaned
      root-strewn   orbs

shaken of   paper skins
      Who is conceived   by the holy
          is born of the virgin

field scented   with the unburied —

[*Épître d'Othéa*, BnF, fr. 606, fol. 11v.]

Latona   denied refuge

banished wanderer   who carried her children
inside her   twinned

mother of light *&* the huntress

delivered on an island   unmoored
between the olive   *&* the palm

upturned   surrounded by swans —
daughter of brightness   *&* the celestial

axis   heaven revolves
around a question

of a woman   robbed

of *terra firma*   labors
nine days *&* nine darknesses

assailed by thirst   *&* raucous
insult   *Who troubles the clear waters*

before her parched petition? Hear now
the sound of night —

village   throats   swollen with venom

[*Épître d'Othéa*, BnF, fr. 606, fol. 15r.]

Io directs the scriptorium

daughter of a river   seized
by a cloud   celestial scepter

her taker   made of her
a gift   horn-polished thick-lashed

an alphabet
of sweet nourishment

at her bidding the apprentices write

a packet of letters   carried on wings
by captive messenger

she leaves   the ribbon untied
inside the ivory chest

a thousand eyes cannot read
what they will not see

her hoof-scratched name —

Watch in whatever place you may be
you do not become sleepy from the sound of flutes

your head separated from its body

[*Épître d'Othéa*, BnF, fr. 606, fol. 46r.]

The Sibyl instructs the emperor

wisdom does not consider
who speaks   but what is said

does not take heed   of what is known
but how much remains

A good ear will hear   wisdom with all desire

as she who spurns the sun
will not flinch to burn her books

before wealth who pays not
their fair-filled worth —

this is how

a fist of sand   oysters a pearl
inside the voice-shattered   ampoule

ten thousand years   becomes
prophet   becomes bridge

& so he learned   from a woman
who taught him about being worshiped

[*The Rape of Philomela by Tereus*, 1562 engraving by Virgil Solis for Ovid's *Metamorphosis*, Book VI 519-562, fol. 80 r.]

Saint Christine   spits her tongue   in the tyrant's face

ripped at   the root   the *radix*

speaks the name   of my mistress   who speaks blasphemy

of a king who steals offerings   from a pure mouth

who belongs to God   the drowning becomes baptism   root-

sprung name   across water   into the cauldron   fired with pitch

& oil   iron hooks wield   sweet melodies —

My namesake   mistress   suspended by her hair   golden-rooted

a bell   who calls   the village women   against a false judge

who terrified   cuts her down   that her tongue commands   evil

from the idol   cast into dust — three thousand men

now speak her name   the immovable body   placed again

into flame   asp & adder bow their heads   vipers clasp her breasts

Severed   the holy name of my mistress   gives not blood

but sweet nourishment   eternal crown & palm —   she voices

heaven   as the mangled root   quivers   a serpent   writhes

the ancient crime   sister of my   speechless mistress   who weaves

scarlet fabric   in another telling a king   devours his own seed   roots

over centuries   in her tongue   puts out the eye   of one

who   does not believe

For a small bell   often sounds   the wise

awake   —

My mistress sings the triumph of the Maid
Le Ditié de Jehanne d'Arc

1]   Je   Christine

        enclosed because of treachery

    I begin now   to laugh

2]   I will change   my language

        from weeping   to singing

    I have well endured   my share

3]   The sun brings back   the good new

    season   I no longer grieve

        I see   what I desire

4]   dry land   green

5]   The cast out child   who suffered

        rose   as a crowned   king

            wearing   spurs of gold

6]   Let us celebrate

        let us all go   great & small —

    may no one hold back   praising God

7]   I won't omit   anything

8]   May it be of value   to those
    Fortune has beaten down

9]   Fortune is always changing
        in whom hope   lives on

10]   Who has seen
        something extraordinary   changed
    from evil   to great good

11]   & truly   through such a miracle
    no one would believe it —

12]   Divine proof   never erred   in faith

13]   You who waged a great war
    see how   your renown is exalted

14]   Your country   you were losing   you have
                    recovered it —

21]   And you   blessed Maid
       you   undid the rope

61] *This poem was inscribed by Christine*
in the aforesaid year 1429
on the day that ends July.
But I expect some discontent
with what it contains,
for who searches with
bowed head & downcast eyes
cannot   regard the light.

Here ends a most beautiful poem composed by Christine.

[*The Romance of Alexander*, BL Royal B XX f. 76v. Origin, Paris.)]

« missives »

[Carried aloft by griffins]

My Mistress tells me
        of eagle-headed lions   fastened by chains   fed with lances
        so travels   the emperor in his cage —
Of my voyage she says   it was the ship
        of an angel   wing sick   over currents   hair shorn
        pilgrim flask   She offered sea monsters elixir
in exchange   for my passage   *Save me O God for the waters   come in*
        even unto my soul   For five seasons   I did not speak
One day   my hand wrote   her tellings
        & every day after —

[Folded into her chest a letter]

contains the hand of her beloved
  who guided
her hand as mistress guides mine
  she does not know I scribe
now a story she did not
      tell me

   *

His hand over my mouth
  the oldest language
speaking nothing
    I returned
watering buckets empty my sister
  read my face readied me
      this journey

   *

Inside the wall buried coins
over weeks over years over eyes
  placed each time
his liege rode to my sister
    she saved for me

        *

My mistress says   night   does not

      reveal a moon   hidden in newness

the dark   welcomes madness   sinners

     thieves

              all those   who flee —

[« Aurora », *Épître d'Othéa*, BnF, fr. 606, fol. 21v.]

[wind-tousled forest   you]

bring me   word   of my ocean

timbered canopies   wave
the sky   like ships

aloft   in a meadow   of long
dew-matted   grasses

where are the caws   of gulls?

~

we arrived by boat   carried on a dark
current   green   the color of
illness   or birth

along the river
my shorn hair   a lamentation   of swans

~

dearest   all days
awaken early   autumn
in the garden   ripe apples   fall to the ground

~

this day I passed
a stand of young aspens   high trunks spearing
countless   triangles of leaves   silvered by the sun

~
scarlet ivy   crosses
the stone wall   like dawn
who   when her hour comes

bestows   *great joy to others*
but within herself holds   sadness &   weeping

[Dearest　　　light]

       breaks　　　　the morning　　pearl

there is　　　much work　　before noon

       widens into none : :

           the goats　　the hay　　　the fire

today　mistress says　we will make

       ink　　　　it brings me to you　　—

              your m　across the sea

ENVOI

LXII   lxii

Je vois   My voice
Jouer.   plays hide & seek

Au bois   In the woods
Je vois.   I search

Pour nois   For us —
Trouver   Finding
Je vois.   Music   I sing

[A little song turned   rhapsodic]

      so that I would not miss

too much   the past   my mistress

    promised   she would   visit

*

each time   music plays

    I hear her voice   singing

*

      &c; when most desolate

    to search   in the spoke of

Fortune's wheel

*

    where music is housed

        there compose

the accompaniment

*

larkspur   aster   snapdragon

    all the blue   of her robe

        woven   into chaplets

*

                                    the wind   circles
round us   an enclave
          of two   ardent furious
ground   whirled   to air
                              *

a knight   rides crusades
           chainmail   across his chest
                                        &   by
          his hand   a sword
                              *

                              syncopation
                       of dances
          my mistress   plays
                              *

                       music heard only
by a family   of daughters
                              *

            she promises   my voice
                       will return
one day —

[Christine presents her book to the Queen, BL Harley MS 4431, fol. 3r.]

Preſence : f. *Preſence; th'aſpect, ſight, or countenance.*
   En la preſence de. *Before, before the face, or eyes; in the verie eye of; he himſelfe, &c, being by.*
   Droict de preſence. *Looke vnder* Droict.
Preſent : m. *A preſent, gift, offer.*
Preſent : m. ente : f. *Preſent; readie; in ſight, in view; at hand, hard by; in preſence, in his owne perſon.*
   `A tous preſents, & à venir. *To all that are and ſhall be; to all aliue and like to be.*
   Par ces preſentes. *By theſe preſents, or preſent letters;* Par la preſente. *By th'inſtant.*
   Par le preſent. *Now, for this time, at this ſeaſon.*
Preſentation : f. *A preſentation; a preſenting, ſhewing, repreſenting, ſetting forth.*

« Before the face, or eyes; A present, gift, offering; To all that have & shall be; to all alive & like to be; A presentation, a presenting, setting forth. »

~

Copied from Randle Cotgrave's
French-English Dictionary, 1611
on this day

of a future century

by a scribe of
Christine

[« Commencement Walk: Mother & Scholar »]

for my students
& teachers

with love, gratitude, & poetry

ACKNOWLEDGEMENTS

In the way of all endeavors across genres, XENO » GLOSSIA relied on collaborative wisdom, and it would not have come into being without the exemplary scholarship, kind encouragement, and generous support of countless individuals, many of whom are listed in the bibliography that follows. Of the authors represented there, I expressly thank the warm community of Christine scholars who welcomed a poet into the fold during the International Christine de Pizan colloquium in Louvain-la-Neuve. Special thanks to the North American Branch of the International Christine de Pizan Society for the award of a Charity Cannon Willard scholarship. May this work pay tribute to Willard's pioneering scholarship and her lifelong collaboration with Sumner Willard, whose translation of *The Book of Deeds of Arms and of Chivalry* served as the generative text for the sequence of erasures, « leavings ». Additional erasures include translations by Jane Chance ("The imagined goddess gives her letter to the young warrior"); Renate Blumenfeld-Kosinski ("My Mistress Sings the Triumph of the Maid"); and Kevin Brownlee ("Here is told how she lost the master of her ship").

Profound gratitude to the University of Southern California; the Dana and David Dornsife College of Letters, Arts and Sciences; the USC Department of English, and the USC PhD Program in Literature and Creative Writing for invaluable support. Special thanks to the USC chapter of Phi Kappa Phi and to the Andrew W. Mellon Foundation and USC Mellon Program in the Humanities and the University of the Future. I am indebted to treasured mentors, Susan McCabe and David St. John, who served not only as guides, but as exemplars of a life in poetry and scholarship. Kind Trojan appreciation to: Emily Anderson, Amy Braden, Alain Borer, Joseph Dane, Richard Fliegel, Mark Irwin, Peter Mancall, Béatrice Mousli, Flora Ruiz, and Sophia Lesinska, whose patient library assistance helped me locate resources far and near (sometimes right under my nose). The incomparable Janalynn Bliss offered North Star guidance along with the beautiful "Commencement Walk" photograph; and my program colleagues, the brilliance of a thousand suns. I extend thanks to the talented cadre of USC composers, musicians, and vocalists who translated poems from « tours » into gorgeous musical form. And to the USC undergraduates who have shared their curiosity, passion, and brilliance in class and on the page over the years: May this work expand the field of what is possible through language; thank you for trusting me with yours.

Alliances forged along the journey include those made in (and on the way to and from) Tours, Paris, Strasbourg, and Marnay-sur-Seine, France, with fond appreciation to the Centre Linguistique Pour Étrangers, l'École des Beaux Arts, the University of Strasbourg, and the Camac Art Centre for hosting inspiration and friendships across continents. Closer to home, heartfelt gratitude to the Napa Valley Writers' Conference and the Community of Writers, which supported « rêves » with a Hillary Gravendyk Memorial Scholarship. Special thanks to: Sarah Wilma Watson, whose gracious invitation to the University of Pennsylvania bridged critical and creative shores; Taije Silverman and Sarah Stickney for spirited conversation at Kelly Writers House; Genevieve Kaplan, who invited talk of « venditions » to the Pacific Ancient Modern Language Association; the many radiant friends of the American Literary Translators Association; and the stellar poet-translators who engaged in further inquiry as part of the "Poetics of the Étrangère" commentary series, at *Jacket2*. I am ever grateful to editors Julia Bloch and Jessica Lowenthal for the opportunity to share conversations about language and interconnection. Sincere thanks to the editors who published portions of this work, sometimes in different forms in the following journals: *The Account*; *Drunken Boat; The Elephants*; *Matter Monthly*; *SWWIM; USC Outstanding Academic Papers by Students.*

Grateful acknowledgment is made to the British Library Board, the Bibliothèque nationale de France, the Getty Research Institute, the Huntington Library, Early English Books Online, HathiTrust Digital Library, USC Libraries, *The Making of the Queen's Manuscript*, Greg Lindahl, and Dutton's Books for sources of illustrative material. Mindful care has been taken to contact copyright holders; should there be any error in attribution or use, the author will make all good-faith effort to remedy it. Gratitude beyond measure to Jon Thompson and David Blakesley for welcoming XENO » GLOSSIA to Parlor Press, to Fran Chapman for keen-eyed reading of the manuscript, and to Dan Beachy-Quick, Cynthia Hogue, Lynn Melnick, and Peter Figen for cheering its entry into the world.

I thank Fortune for the sustaining love of dear ones and pay particular homage to the women of my family. Of the generations that came before, I have the privilege of knowing these names: Dora Friedman, Lena Hennes, Leanora Miller, Jeanette Jacobs, Gloria Rappaport, Darlyene Greenberg, Doris Betty Miller, Anne Hennes, Barbara Vogel, and Dr. Lillian Brown Vogel, who set me on a scholar's course with inspiration and a terrific vote of confidence. To my own beautiful mother, Ilene Estelle Enz: An entire universe of thanks for gifts over a lifetime, and beyond. Following the lead of Christine's remarkable *pioche*, I channel deep wells of gratitude to untold others—neighbors, strangers, and beloveds whose presence, kindnesses, and poetries lighted a true path of learning. May the teachings ignited by Christine continue far into a future of which we can only dream.

BIBLIOGRAPHY

WORKS BY CHRISTINE DE PIZAN

The Book of Deeds of Arms and of Chivalry. Trans. Sumner Willard. Ed. Charity Cannon Willard. University Park: Pennsylvania State University Press, 1999.

The Book of Peace by Christine de Pizan. Trans. and ed. Karen Green, Constant J. Mews, Janice Pindar, and Tania van Hemelryck. University Park: Pennsylvania State University Press, 2007.

The Book of the Body Politic. Ed. and trans. Kate Langdon Forhan. Cambridge University Press, 1994.

The Book of the City of Ladies. Trans. E. J. Richards. New York: Persea, 1982. See also the translation by Rosalind Brown-Grant. London: Penguin, 1999.

The Book of the Mutability of Fortune. Ed and trans. Geri Smith. Tempe: Arizona Center for Medieval & Renaissance Studies, 2017.

The Book of the Duke of True Lovers. Trans. Thelma S. Fenster. New York: Persea Books, 1991.

Le Chemin de Longue Étude. Trans. and ed. Andrea Tarnowski. Paris: Librairie Générale Française, 2000.

Debate of the "Romance of the Rose." Ed. and trans. David F. Hult. Chicago: University of Chicago Press, 2010.

Ditié de Jehanne d'Arc. Ed. Angus J. Kennedy and Kenneth Varty. Oxford: Medium Aevum Monographs, 1977.

The Epistle of Othea to Hector, or The Boke of Knyghthode, Translated from the French of Cristine de Pisan by Stephen Scrope. Ed. George F. Warner. London: J.B. Nichols and Sons, 1904. Online through HathiTrust and the Getty Research Institute.

Letter of Othea to Hector. Trans. and ed. Jane Chance. Newburyport, MA: Focus Information Group, 1990.

Othea's Letter to Hector. Trans and ed. Renate Blumenfeld-Kosinski and Earl Jeffrey Richards. New York: Iter Press, 2017.

The morale prouerbes of Cristyne. Trans. Anthony Woodville, Earl Rivers. London: Caxton, 1478. Reproduction of original in the Henry E. Huntington Library and Art Gallery.

Œuvres poétiques de Christine de Pisan. Ed. Maurice Roy. 3 vols. Paris: Librairie de Firmin Didot et Cie: 1884-96. Online through Project Gutenberg.

The Selected Writings of Christine de Pizan. Ed. Renate Blumenfeld-Kosinski. Trans. Renate Blumenfeld-Kosinski and Kevin Brownlee. New York: W.W. Norton, 1997.

The Writings of Christine de Pizan. Selected and Edited by Charity Cannon Willard. Trans. Charity Cannon Willard et al. New York: Persea, 1994.

The Vision of Christine de Pizan. Trans. Glenda K. McLeod and Charity Cannon Willard. Cambridge: D.S. Brewer, 2005.

ANTECEDENTS, CONTEMPORARIES, DESCENDENTS, KINSHIPS

Boccaccio, Giovanni. *Famous Women*. Ed. and trans. Virginia Brown. Cambridge: Harvard University Press, 2001.

Boethius. *The Consolation of Philosophy*. Trans. Scott Goins and Barbara H. Wyman. San Francisco: Ignatius Press, 2012.

Bonet [Bovet], Honoré. *The Tree of Battles*. Trans. G.W. Coopland. Cambridge: Harvard University Press, 1949.

Bourgeois de Paris. *Journal d'un Bourgeois de Paris*. Trans. Janet Shirley. Oxford: Oxford University Press, 1968.

D'Aulaires's Book of Greek Myths. Ingri and Edgar Parin D'aulaire, New York: Delacorte, 1962.

The Danse Macabre of Women [Ms. BnF, fr. 995 BnF]. Ed. and trans. Ann Tukey Harrison. Kent: Kent State University Press, 1994.

Dante Alighieri. *The Divine Comedy*. Trans. John D. Sinclair. New York: Oxford University Press, 1961. See also translation by Mary Jo Bang, Minneapolis: Graywolf Press, 2012.

The Distaff Gospels: A First Modern English Edition of Les Évangiles des Quenouilles. Trans. and ed. Madeleine Jeay and Kathleen Garay. Ontario: Broadview Editions, 2006.

Froissart, Jean. *Chronicles* [Abridged]. Trans. and ed. Geoffrey Brereton. New York: Penguin, 1978.

The Good Wife's Guide (Le Ménagier de Paris): A Medieval Household Book. Trans. Gina L. Greco and Christine M. Rose. Ithaca: Cornell University Press, 2009.

Guillaume de Lorris and Jean de Meun. *The Romance of the Rose.* Trans. Frances Horgan. Oxford: Oxford University Press, 2009.

Hesiod. *Theogony, Works and Days, Shield.* Trans. and ed. Apostolos N. Athanassakis. Baltimore: Johns Hopkins University Press, 2004.

Joan of Arc: In Her Own Words. Trans. and ed. Willard Trask. New York: Turtlepoint Press, 1996.

Le Fèvre, Jean. *The Book of Gladness/Le Livre de Leesce.* Trans. Linda Burke. Jefferson, NC: McFarland & Co. 2013.

Legano, John of. *Tractatus de bello, de reprisaliis et de duello.* Ed. T.E. Holland. Trans. J.L. Brierly. Oxford: Oxford University Press, 1977.

Machaut, Guillaume de. *Le livre dou voir dit/The book of the true poem.* Ed. Daniel Leech-Wilkinson. Trans. Barton. R. Palmer, New York: Garland Pub., 1998.

Macrobius. *Commentary on the Dream of Scipio.* Trans. William Harris Stahl. New York: Columbia University Press, 1990.

Mandeville, John. *The Travels of Sir John Mandeville.* Trans. C.W.R.D. Moseley. London: Penguin, 2005.

Ovid. *Metamorphoses.* Trans. Charles Martin. Introduction by Bernard Knox. New York: W.W. Norton, 2004.

Tales from Ovid. Trans. Ted Hughes. New York: FSG, 1997.

Vegetius, *Epitome of Military Science.* Trans. N.P. Milner. Liverpool: Liverpool University Press, Translated Texts for Historians. vol. 16, 1993.

CRITICAL & BIOGRAPHICAL WORKS

Adams, Tracy. *Christine de Pizan and the Fight for France.* University Park, PA: Pennsylvania State University Press, 2014.

Altmann, Barbara K. and Deborah L. McGrady. *Christine de Pizan: A Casebook.* New York: Routledge, 2003.

Bell, Susan Groag: *The Lost Tapestries of the City of Ladies: Christine de Pizan's Renaissance Legacy.* Berkeley: University of California Press, 2004.

Blumenfeld-Kosinski, Renate. "Christine de Pizan: Mythographer and Mythmaker." *Reading Myth: Classical Mythology and Its Interpretations in Medieval French Literature*, 171–212. Stanford: Stanford University Press, 1997.

Brownlee, Kevin. "Martyrdom and the Female Voice: Saint Christine in the Cité des dames." *Images of Sainthood in Medieval Europe*, ed. Renate Blumenfeld-Kosinski and Timea Szell Ithaca, 115–35. NY: Cornell University Press, 1991.

Carroll, Berenice. "Christine de Pizan and the Origins of Peace Theory." *Women Writers and the Early Modern British Political Tradition*, ed. Hilda L. Smith, 22–39. Cambridge: Cambridge University Press, 1998.

Cerquiglini, Jacqueline "The Stranger." *The Selected Writings of Christine De Pizan*, ed. Renate Blumenfeld-Kosinski, 265-274. New York: W.W. Norton, 1997.

Chance, Jane. "Re-membering Herself: Christine de Pizan's Refiguration of Isis as Io." *Modern Philology*, 111.2 (2013): 133–57.

Cooper-Davis, Charlotte. *Christine de Pizan: Life, Work, Legacy*. London: Reaction Books, 2021.

DeLamotte, Eugenia C., Natania Meeker, and Jean F. OBarr. "Christine de Pizan." *Women Imagine Change: A Global Anthology of Women's Resistance from 600 B.C.E. to Present*. New York: Routledge, 1997.

Desmond, Marilyn, ed. *Christine de Pizan and the Categories of Difference*. Minneapolis: University of Minnesota Press, 1998.

Desmond, Marilynn and Pamela Sheingorn. *Myth, Montage, & Visuality in Late Medieval Manuscript Culture: Christine de Pizan's Epistre Othea*. Ann Arbor: University of Michigan Press, 2006.

Ferguson, Margaret W. "An Empire of Her Own: Literacy as Appropriation in Christine de Pizan's Livre de la Cité des Dames." *Dido's Daughters: Literacy, Gender, and Empire in Early Modern England and France*, 179–225. University of Chicago Press, 2007.

Green, Karen. "Christine de Pizan: Isolated Individual or Member of a Feminine Community of Learning?" *Communities of Learning: Networks and the Shaping of Intellectual Identity in Europe, 110-1500*, ed. Constant J. Mews and J. N. Crossley, 229–50. Turnhout: Brepols, 2011.

———. "Was Christine de Pizan at Poissy 1418-1429?" *Medium Aevum* 83 (2014): 28–40.

Ignatius, Mary Ann "Christine de Pizan's 'Epistre Othea': An Experiment in Literary Form." *Medievalia et humanistica* 9 (1979): 127–42.

Kelly, Douglas. *Christine de Pizan's Changing Opinion: A Quest for Certainty in the Midst of Chaos*. Cambridge: D.S. Brewer, 2007.

Laidlaw, James. "Christine de Pizan: A Publisher's Progress." *The Modern Language Review* 82, no. 1 (1987): 35–75.

———. "Christine de Pizan, the Earl of Salisbury, and Henry IV." *French Studies* 36 (1982): 129–43.

LeBlanc, Yvonne. "A Diachronic Perspective of the Verse Epistle in the Fifteenth Century (Eustice Deschamps and Christine de Pizan)." *Va Lettre Va: The French Verse Epistle (1400–1500)*, 59-75. Birmingham: Summa, 1995.

Laird, Edgar. "Christine de Pizan and the Controversy Concerning Star-Study in the Court of Charles V." *Allegorica* 18 (1997): 21–30.

Margolis, Nadia. *An Introduction to Christine de Pizan*. Gainesville: University Press of Florida, 2011.

McGrady, Deborah. "Reading for Authority: Portraits of Christine de Pizan and Her Readers." *Author, Reader, Book: Medieval Authorship in Theory and Practice*, ed. Stephen Partridge and Erik Kwakkel, 154–77. Toronto: University of Toronto Press, 2012.

McLeod, Enid. *The Order of the Rose: The Life and Ideas of Christine de Pizan.* Totowa, NJ: Rowman and Littlefield, 1976.

Ouy, Gilbert, Christine Reno and Inès Villela-Petit, Oliver Delsaux, and Tania van Hemelryck. *Album Christine de Pizan.* Turnhout: Brepols, 2012.

Quilligan, Maureen. *The Allegory of Female Authority: Christine de Pizan's Cité des Dames.* Ithaca: Cornell University Press, 1991.

Richards, E. Jeffrey, ed. *Christine de Pizan and Medieval French Lyric.* Gainesville: University Press of Florida, 1998.

_____. "Jean Gerson's Writings to His Sisters and Christine de Pizan's Livre des trois vertus: An Intellectual Dialogue Culminating in Friendship." *Virtue Ethics for Women: 1250-1500*, ed. Karen Green and Constant J. Mews, 81–98. Dordrecht: Springer, 2011.

_____. "The Lady Wants to Talk: Christine de Pizan's Epistre a Eustace Mourel." *Eustache Deschamps, French Courtier-Poet: His Work and His World*, ed. Deborah M. Sinnreich-Levi, 109–122. New York: AMS Press, 1997.

_____. " 'Seulette a part'— The 'Little Woman on the Sidelines' Takes Up Her Pen: The Letters of Christine de Pizan." *Dear Sister: Medieval Women and the Epistolary Genre*, ed. Karen Cherewatuk and Ulrike Wiethaus, 139–70. Philadelphia: University of Pennsylvania Press, 1993.

Richards, E. Jeffrey, with Joan Williamson, Nadia Margolis, and Christine Reno, eds. *Reinterpreting Christine de Pizan.* Athens: University of Georgia Press, 1992.

Shapiro, Norman. "Christine de Pizan." *French Women Poets of Nine Centuries.* Baltimore: Johns Hopkins University Press, 2008.

Walters, Lori. "The Figure of the Seulette in the Works of Christine de Pizan and Jean Gerson." In *Desireuse de plus avant enquerre: Actes du VIe Colloque international sur Christine de Piazn*, ed. Liliane Dulac, Anne Paupert, Christine Reno, and Bernard Ribémont, 119–39. Paris: Champion, 2008.

Willard, Charity Cannon. *Christine de Pizan: Her Life and Works.* New York: Persea, 1984

MEDIEVAL HISTORY, CULTURE, LITERATURE, POLITICS, SOCIETY & BELIEFS

Armstrong, Adrian, Sarah Kay, and Rebecca Dixon. *Knowing Poetry: Verse in Medieval France from The Rose to the Rhétoriqueurs.* Ithaca: Cornell University Press, 2011.

Amt, Emilie. *Women's Lives in Medieval Europe.* New York: Routledge, 2010.

Camille, Michael. *The Medieval Art of Love.* New York: Abrams, 1998.

Coldiron, A.E.B. *Canon, Period, and the Poetry of Charles of Orleans.* Ann Arbor: University of Michigan Press, 2000.

Cooper-Rompato, Christine F. *The Gift of Tongues: Women's Xenoglossia in the Later Middle Ages.* University Park, PA : Pennsylvania State University Press, 2010.

Dronke, Peter. *Verse with Prose From Petronius to Dante: The Art and Scope of the Mixed Form.* Cambridge, MA: Harvard University Press, 1994.

Famiglietti, R.C. *Royal Intrigue: Crisis at the Court of Charles VI, 1392–1420*. New York: AMS Press, 1986.

Goldstone, Nancy. *The Maid and the Queen: The Secret History of Joan of Arc*. New York: Penguin, 2012.

Hasse, Hella S. *In a Dark Wood Wandering: A Novel of the Middle Ages*. Ed. and trans. Anita Miller and Lewis C. Kaplan. Chicago: Academy Chicago Publishers, 1991.

Jager, Eric. *Blood Royal: A True Tale of Crime and Detection in Medieval Paris*. New York: Little, Brown and Company, 2014.

Kelly, Douglas. *Machaut and the Medieval Apprenticeship Tradition: Truth, Fiction and Poetic Craft*. Cambridge: D.S. Brewer, 2014.

Kruger, Steven F. *Dreaming in the Middle Ages*. Cambridge: Cambridge University Press, 1992.

Lewis, C.S. *The Discarded Image*. Cambridge: Cambridge University Press, 1964.

Mortimer, Ian. *The Time Traveler's Guide to Medieval England: A Handbook for Visitors to the Fourteenth Century*. New York: Simon and Schuster, 2008.

Phillips, Helen. "Dream Poems." *A Companion to Medieval English Literature and Culture (c. 1350–1500)*. Ed. Peter Brown. Oxford: Blackwell Publishing, 2007.

Philips, Helen and Nick Havely, Eds. *Chaucer's Dream Poetry*. London: Longman, 1997.

Roux, Simone. *Paris in the Middle Ages*. Trans. Jo Ann McNamera. Philadelphia: University of Pennsylvania Press, 2009.

Smoller, Laura Ackerman Smoller. *History, Prophecy, and the Stars: The Christian Astrology of Pierre D'Ailly, 1350–1420*. Princeton: Princeton University Press, 1994.

A.C. Spearing, A.C. *Medieval Dream-Poetry*. Cambridge: Cambridge University Press, 1976.

Tuchman, Barbara W. *A Distant Mirror: The Calamitous 14th Century*. New York: Random House, 1978.

Ward, Jennifer. *Women in Medieval Europe 1200–1500*. London: Pearson, 2002.

Wilson, Katharina M. and Nadia Margolis. *Women in the Middle Ages: An Encyclopedia*. Westport, CN: Greenwood Press, 2004.

Veenstra, Jan R. *Magic and Divination at the Courts of Burgundy and France*. Leiden: Brill, 1998.

MEDIEVAL MANUSCRIPT CULTURE, PRODUCTION, TEXT, & ILLUMINATION

Battistini, Matilde. *Astrology, Magic, and Alchemy in Art*. Trans. Rosanna M. Giammanco Frongia. Los Angeles: Getty Publications, 2004.

Brown, Michelle P. *Understanding Illuminated Manuscripts: A Guide to Technical Terms*. Los Angeles: Getty Publications, 1994.

DeHamel, Christopher. *Scribes and Illuminators*. Toronto: University of Toronto Press, 1992.

Hedeman, Anne D. *The Royal Image: Illustrations of the Grandes Chroniques de France, 1274–1422*. Berkeley: University of California Press, 1991.

Hindeman, Sandra. *Christine de Pizan's "Epistre Othéa": Painting and Politics at the Court of Charles VI*. Toronto: Pontifical Institute of Mediaeval Studies, 1986.

Kempf, Damien and Maria L. Gilbert. *Medieval Monsters*. London: The British Library, 2015.

Meiss, Millard. *French Painting in the Time of Jean de Berry*. 2 Volumes. London: Pahidon, 1967.

Morrison, Elizabeth. *Beasts: Factual and Fantastic*. Los Angeles: Getty Publications, 2007.

Morrison, Elizabeth and Anne D. Hedeman, eds. *Imagining the Past in France: History in Manuscript Painting 1250–1500*. Los Angeles: Getty Publications, 2010.

Page, Sophie. *Astrology in Medieval Manuscripts*. Toronto: University of Toronto Press, 2002.

Porter, Pamela. *Courtly Love in Medieval Manuscripts*. Toronto: University of Toronto Press, 2003.

_____. *Medieval Warfare in Medieval Manuscripts*. Toronto: University of Toronto Press, 2000.

Rouse, Richard H. and Mary A. *Manuscripts and Their Makers: Commercial Book Producers in Medieval Paris 1220–1500*. Turnhout, Belgium: Harvey Miller Publishers, 2000.

REGARDING LANGUAGE & TRANSLATION

Benjamin, Walter. "The Task of the Translator." *Illuminations*. Trans. Harry Zohn. Ed Hannah Arendt. New York: Schocken Books, 1968.

Carson, Anne. "Variations on the Right to Remain Silent." *Float*. New York: Knopf, 2016.

Hejinian, Lyn. "Forms in Alterity: On Translation." *The Language of Inquiry*. Berkeley: University of California Press, 2000.

Old French-English Dictionary. Eds. Alan Hindley, Frederick W. Langley, and Brian J. Levy. Cambridge: Cambridge University Press, 2000.

Oxford English Dictionary Online.

Ricoeur, Paul. *On Translation*. Trans. Eileen Brennan. Intro. Richard Kearney. London & New York: Routledge, 2006.

Schulte, Rainer and John Biguenet, Ed. *Theories of Translation*. Chicago: University of Chicago Press, 1992.

Spivak, Gayatri Chakravorty. "The Politics of Translation." *Outside in the Teaching Machine*, 179–200. New York: Routledge, 1993.

Swensen, Cole. *Noise that Stays Noise: Essays*. Ann Arbor: University of Michigan Press, 2014.

FURTHER ILLUMINATIONS: TEXTUAL, VISUAL, VIRTUAL

The Art of Alchemy. Exhibition of the Getty Research Institute. Los Angeles, CA. October 11, 2016–February 12, 2017.

Bachelard, Gaston. *The Poetics of Reverie: Childhood, Language, and the Cosmos*. Trans. Daniel Russell. Boston: Beacon Press, 1960.

Bergvall, Caroline. *Meddle English*. New York: Nightboat Books, 2001.

Bonnefoy, Yves. *The Act and the Place of Poetry*. Ed. and trans. by John T. Naughton. Chicago: The University of Chicago Press, 1989.

British Library Digital Catalogue of Illuminated Manuscripts.

Carson, Anne. *Plainwater*. New York: Vintage, 1995.

Cha, Theresa Hak Kyung. *Dictee*. Berkeley: University of California Press, 2001.

Christine de Pizan Digital Scriptorium. Joint project of the University of Waterloo, Sheridan Libraries of Johns Hopkins University, and the Bibliothèque nationale de France. Online.

Christine de Pizan: The Making of the Queen's Manuscript [British Harley MS 4431]. Collaborative project under the direction of James Laidlaw, University of Edinburgh. Online.

Cixous, Hélène. "Coming to Writing." *Coming to Writing and Other Essays*. Ed. Deborah Jenson. Trans. Deborah Jenson. Cambridge, MA: Harvard University Press, 1991.

_____. *Dream I Tell You*. Trans. Beverley Bie Brahic. New York: Columbia University Press, 2006.

_____ . "The School of Dreams." *Three Steps on the Ladder of Writing*. Trans. Sarah Cornell and Susan Sellers, 55–108. New York: Columbia University Press, 1993.

Debord, Guy. "Theory of the Dérive." Trans. Ken Knabb. *Les Lèvres Nues* #9 November, 1956. Accessed at the *Situationist International Online*, March 15, 2016.

Gallica Digital Library of the Bibliothèque nationale de France.

Glissant, Édouard. *Poetic Intention*. Trans. Nathalie Stephens. Callicoon: Nightboat Books, 1997.

Hejinian, Lyn. *The Language of Inquiry*. Berkeley: University of California Press, 2000.

Howe, Susan. *My Emily Dickinson*. New York: New Directions, 2007 (1985).

Jung, Carl. *The Red Book*. New York: W.W. Norton, 2009.

Kaplan, S.C. and Sarah Wilma Watson. *Books of Duchesses: Mapping Women Book Owners, 1350–1550*. Online.

Kearney, Richard and Kascha Semonovitch, eds. *Phenomenologies of the Stranger: Between Hostility and Hospitality*. New York: Fordham University Press, 2011.

Kristeva, Julia. *Strangers to Ourselves*. New York: Columbia University Press, 1991.

Musée national du Moyen Âge (Cluny Museum). Paris, France.

Ramazani, Jahan. *Poetry and Its Others: News, Prayer, Song and the Dialogue of Genres*. Chicago: University of Chicago Press, 2014.

Rilke, Rainer Maria. *The Notebooks of Malte Laurids Brigge*. Trans. M.D. Herter Norton. New York: W.W. Norton, 1949.

Quoi de neuf au Moyan Âge? Exhibition of Le Cité des sciences et de l'industrie. Paris, France. October 11, 2016–June 10, 2017.

Risset, Jacqueline. *Sleep's Powers*. Trans. Jennifer Moxley. Brooklyn: Ugly Duckling Press, 2008.

Tarnowski, Andrea, Ed. *Approaches to Teaching the Works of Christine de Pizan*. New York: Modern Language Association, 2018.

ABOUT THE AUTHOR

Marci Vogel is a first-generation scholar, poet, translator, and educator. She is author of *Death and Other Holidays* (Melville House, 2018), winner of the Miami Book Fair / de Groot Prize for the Novella, and *At the Border of Wilshire & Nobody*, selected for the inaugural Howling Bird Press Poetry Prize. Her work has received support from the Community of Writers, the Napa Valley Writers' Conference, and the Camargo Foundation. The recipient of a Willis Barnstone Translation Prize, her commentary series on translation and poetics is archived at *Jacket2*. Vogel holds a PhD in Literature and Creative Writing from the University of Southern California, where she served as a Mellon Postdoctoral Fellow in the Humanities and the University of the Future.

www.ingramcontent.com/pod-product-compliance
Lightning Source LLC
Chambersburg PA
CBHW061127010526
44116CB00023B/2996